ABOUT THE AUTHOR:

GEORGE FOOSHEE, JR., a graduate
of Southern Methodist University and a
Phi Beta Kappa, holds a Masters in Business Administration from Harvard Business School. President of a credit agency,
Mr. Fooshee is an experienced counselor
and lecturer in the area of biblical principles of personal finance. He is actively involved in church work in Wichita, Kansas, where he lives with his wife and two
daughters.

YOU CAN BE

FINANCIALLY FREE

YOU CAN BE
FINANCIALLY FREE

GEORGE FOOSHEE, JR.

Fleming H. Revell Company

Old Tappan, New Jersey

Scripture quotations, unless otherwise identified, are from The Living Bible, Copyright © 1971 by Tyndale House Publishers, Wheaton, Illinois 60187. All rights reserved.

Scripture quotations identified KJV are from the King James Version of the Bible.

Scripture quotations identified NEB are from The New English Bible. © The Delegates of the Oxford University Press and the Syndics of the Cambridge University Press 1961 and 1970. Reprinted by permission.

Scripture quotations identified RSV are from the Revised Standard Version of the Bible, copyrighted 1946, 1952, © 1971 and 1973.

Scripture quotations identified PHILLIPS are from THE NEW TESTAMENT IN MODERN ENGLISH (Revised Edition), translated by J. B. Phillips. © J. B. Phillips 1958, 1960, 1972. Used by permission of Macmillan Publishing Co., Inc.

Quotations from the radio program #2346, "Start Late, Stay Late," are reprinted with permission of the Nightingale-Conant Corporation, Chicago, 1974 copyright, producers of the Earl Nightingale Radio Program, "Our Changing World."

The Family Life Cycle chart is used by permission. James L. Allen, Managing Editor, *Today's Consumer, A Semester Course in Consumer Education,* Homemaking Research Laboratories, Tony, Wisconsin, 1971.

The cartoons in Chapter 6 are used by permission of the artist, Carla J. Brown.

Library of Congress Cataloging in Publication Data

Fooshee, George, Jr.
    You can be financially free.

    1. Finance, Personal. 2. Stewardship, Christian.
I. Title.
HG179.F57   332'.024   76-1025
ISBN 0-8007-0790-7

Acknowledgments

Many friends have prayed for and encouraged me as I have written this book. Several have made exceptional contributions, and I am thankful to acknowledge them by name.

My wife, Marjean, has shared this vision with me and has been a constant encourager. She also has shared the keeping of the financial records throughout our marriage.

Ford Madison was patiently discipling me during the germination and fulfillment of the vision for this book.

Gene Warr persistently checked on my progress with regular reminders of the need for useful material on personal finance.

Max Barnett provided many opportunities for these principles to be tested with young audiences.

Jane Fite, my secretary, has not only typed each page several times but also has been a regular tiger on the details.

My college roommate, Richard Wilke, spent hours reading the manuscript with me, offering helpful changes.

And Roger Palms of *Decision* magazine suggested ways to edit the material to its present size.

To these, and a host of others who have made such positive contributions, I thank the Lord for each of you.

And may God have all the glory!

Contents

Preface

The purpose of this book is to present clearly and simply from the Scriptures the principles God has established for money. Three areas of personal finances are presented:

Sharing—"For if you give, you will get! . . ."

Luke 6:38

Spending—". . . be content with what you have. . . ."

Hebrews 13:5 RSV

Saving—"The wise man saves for the future. . . ."

Proverbs 21:20

Why all this emphasis on money for the Christian? Since the Bible speaks about money so often, the Christian must listen. To be in harmony with God—to receive the blessings He has for us and to be used for His good purposes—we Christians must know and obey God's money principles.

If you are not a Christian, you still can profit from an awareness of clear financial principles. Decisions about money matters have far-reaching and cumulative effects on your present life-style as well as on your future choices. Some decisions now may save you thousands of dollars in your lifetime—dollars which may have great meaning to your family during a crisis or an opportunity.

Knowledge of and obedience to God's money principles are frequently lacking. Ask any minister how often money worries are present in marital counseling. My own experience indicates that financial pressures and tensions exist in most marriages. Many couples would rather be mired in debt than face the trauma of working through to agreement on the family budget and then keeping records to check their progress. Singles fail just as easily in their money management, with the resultant crop of frustration and despair.

God's Way is the "narrow gate" that is hard, but His Way leads to *abundant life*. The world's way in money is the "easy payment" way —so easy and so wide—but it leads to destruction! The fruits of the easy way are bills, payments, interest, pressure, and financial bondage. As one minister who was trying to climb up the long trail out of debt wrote, "We are getting our debts whittled down, but it sure is slower than it was in getting into them." Many of you who read this book will be able to shout "Amen" to that!

Why look to the Bible for information about installment loans, revolving charge accounts, mortgage payments, budgeting, investments, and the intricacies of personal finances? Aren't these financial complexities all products of a modern credit system which was developed long after the Bible was written?

Not really! The "easy payment" methods of going broke fast are relatively new, but God's established principles for money are timeless—and are as relevant today as His simple eternal message of salvation, "Repent, and believe in the gospel" (*see* Mark 1:15 RSV).

My prayer for you is that you will learn and apply these financial principles to your life so that you will experience God's best in the wise use of your money.

YOU CAN BE

FINANCIALLY FREE

1 The Debt Trap

FLY NOW! PAY LATER!

Sounds easy. And fun! Consider these slogans widely used on TV, billboards, and in direct-mail advertising:

PRESENTING: THE BEST FRIEND YOUR CHECKING ACCOUNT EVER HAD.

INTRODUCING: THE "PEACE OF MIND" CHECKING ACCOUNT.

NOW: AN EASY SOLUTION TO TAX AND INSURANCE PROBLEMS.

These friendly phrases have been used by bank credit-card companies to promote the uses of their plastic cards. What are these painless answers to your financial problems? Have these credit-card companies discovered some slick way for you to spend more money than you have in your checking account?

NO! NO!! NO!!!

They are presenting you with so-called convenience checks. When you want to spend more than you have, you simply fill out your convenience check. Instantly you have secured what they call a cash advance. The check you have written has been an instant addition to your bank credit-card account. You have borrowed that money at an annual percentage rate of 18%. The BEST FRIEND, the EASY SOLUTION, the PEACE OF MIND add up to one word which the advertising neglects to mention: DEBT!

What's so bad about debt? Isn't everybody in hock? Don't companies owe money? Isn't virtually every city and state government liable for millions of dollars? Isn't our federal government constantly raising the legal debt limit a few more billion dollars? Aren't most churches involved in debt? What's the catch?

The catch is that debt is a trap. A *trap* can be defined as: anything that attracts because it seems easy but proves to be difficult. How true that is for *debt*.

The debt trap has a way of accelerating at a fearful pace. Observe in Table 1 the history of the Federal Budget Deficit and the steady increases in the average deficits during recent five-year periods.

Table 1: Federal Budget Deficit

Five-Year Period	Average Deficit (Billions)
1951–1955	$ 1.2
1956–1960	1.6
1961–1965	4.6
1966–1970	7.5
1971–1975	17.5

Consider Larry, a Christian brother, who related this sad story in my office. He had married at the age of sixteen with no knowledge of financial affairs. After seventeen years of marriage he found that he had learned very little about money. Recently divorced but now remarried, his monthly payments on house, cars, furniture, and signature loans now totaled $586; his net monthly income was $594. Is

BLONDIE®   By Chic Young

© King Features Syndicate 1972.

this the *abundant life?* Or is this the inevitable reaping of careless overspending?

Didn't Jesus tell us that He came that we may have life and that we may have it more abundantly? (*See* John 10:10 KJV.) Doesn't the abundant life mean having what you want when you want it? Doesn't the abundant life mean new cars, color television, air conditioning, stereo, several bathrooms, and stylish clothes for each season?

Some families who have come to me for counseling have discovered the pitfalls of such abundance when the foundation for their possessions is built on debt. In this group were two ministers, one top executive, a salesman, a professional man, and a divorcee. All were Christians seeking a closer walk with Christ. Yet one man's job was threatened because of his financial predicament. Another man had recently been hospitalized for several days, having succumbed emotionally to the debt pressures bearing upon him. Although these six had incomes ranging from under $10,000 to over $36,000 per year, they all had two things in common. They were all deeply in debt; and they all had learned the reality of this little jingle:

> THAT MONEY TALKS
> I'LL NOT DENY.
> I HEARD IT ONCE.
> IT SAID, GOOD-BYE.

What is debt? A usual definition is that *debt* is something owed to another. There is a sense of obligation on the part of the borrower to pay back the debt to the lender. The word *lend* means to let another have or use for a time. When the time is up, the money is expected to be repaid. In the meantime, the borrower is living in a second state—the state of debt. Now he's a member of the "debt set."

Why do those who sell easy credit fail to use the word *debt* in their ads? Why are the adjectives commonly used for debt left out of descriptions of the new state into which you move when you borrow money? When I looked at all the adjectives listed for *debt* in *Roget's College Thesaurus,* I quickly understood the reasons:

indebted; liable, chargeable, answerable for, in debt, in embarrassed circumstances; in difficulties; encumbered, involved; involved in debt, plunged in debt; deep in debt; deeply involved; up against it; in the red; fast tied up; insolvent; minus, out of pocket; unpaid; unrequited, unrewarded; owing, due, in arrears, outstanding. *Slang,* in hock, on the cuff.

Were you uncomfortable as you saw this list? Did you notice the negative aspects of each word and phrase used to describe *debt?*

A mother whose spelling was weak unintentionally described the pit of debt in a letter to our office. She said, "We are quite a bit in depth."

Debt in God's economy is an excess of liabilities over assets. A home, if financed conservatively, may usually be sold for more than is owed by the mortgagor. A car, or furniture, or most any depreciating item purchased on time cannot usually be sold for sufficient money to pay off the lender. Ask any credit union or bank how they come out financially when goods are repossessed. My experience is that repossession is usually a financial disaster for both the borrower and the lender.

A good rule for borrowing is: Never borrow to buy depreciating items. Such things as cars, furniture, clothes, appliances, boats, and luxury items should not be purchased until money is available to pay for them. The family home is a special situation and will be considered in another chapter.

The world offers another sneaky way of plunging a person into the debt trap. This sinister method is called *cosigning.* People who cosign feel that they are doing a relative or friend a favor. The potential cost of their signature is usually not explained very carefully to them. In a given situation the cosigner may feel some embarrassment at quizzing the lender about what will happen if his relative or friend does not pay as he has promised. The Scriptures warn us to avoid cosigning:

> Son, if you endorse a note for someone you hardly know, guaranteeing his debt, you are in serious trouble. You may have trapped yourself by your agreement. Quick! Get out of it if you possibly can! Swallow your pride; don't let embarrassment stand in the way. Go and beg to have your name erased. Don't put it off. Do it now.

Don't rest until you do. If you can get out of this trap you have saved yourself like a deer that escapes from a hunter, or a bird from the net.

Proverbs 6:1–5

Let me explain what you are doing if you cosign a note. I want you to understand the financial transaction in which you would involve yourself. Here are three steps:

You are borrowing the money.   The lender has refused to make the loan to the person for whom you are cosigning. His decision has been based on facts which reveal that the risk is too great to loan the money to your friend or relative. When you sign the note, the money is really being loaned to you. The reason you have been asked to sign is because your collateral, your character, your credit, and your capacity are sufficient for him to feel good about his security on the loan. Your signature is his security.

You are loaning the money you borrowed to a person who was too great a risk for the professional lender.   You are involving yourself in a business transaction that the expert money manager wouldn't touch.

You are hoping that your friend or relative will pay back the loan. I can tell you he probably won't. My friends who are bankers tell me that approximately 50% of all cosigners end up paying.

When your friend or relative defaults, then you have the "privilege" of paying back the money. It's been my experience that cosigners seldom plan on this repayment. I have also witnessed much bitterness in the lives of people over the repayment of such agreements. One of the reasons, I believe, that God counsels us against cosigning is because of the destructive potential in a human relationship that often results from this kind of financial transaction.

Whenever you cosign you are violating God's commandment to keep out of debt. You have assumed the debt of another. That's just another way to enter the state of debt.

Is it any wonder that God, always so positive, gives three reasons for avoiding debt?

Debt violates God's commandment for our lives.   "Keep out of debt altogether . . ." (Romans 13:8 PHILLIPS). God says KEEP OUT! The sign is clear. Keeping out of debt certainly isn't easy. But the Bible gives a definite way to avoid the trap—"make do with your pay!" (*see* Luke 3:14 NEB). Individuals I know in the debt trap took exactly the same road to get there—they spent more money than they made. They violated the commandment to be content with their wages by overspending their income. The Talmud has wise counsel for our spending: "A man should always eat and drink less than his means allow, clothe himself in accordance with his means, and honour his wife and children more than his means allow."

Debt is costly.   Why are so many people blind to the pitfalls of easy credit? They do not count *the cost*. The Bible instructs: "But don't begin until you count the cost. For who would begin construction of a building without first getting estimates and then checking to see if he has enough money to pay the bills?" (Luke 14:28).

What is the cost of debt for a family earning $12,000 annually and consistently overspending its income by $1,000 a year, or a seemingly small amount of $83.33 each month? The cost of plunging into debt at this rate, for 10 years, is revealed in Table 2. Assume the interest rate is 10%.

Table 2: Cost of Debt Accumulation

Year	Amount Borrowed	Total Debt	Interest Paid
1	$ 1,000	$ 1,000	$ 100
2	1,000	2,000	200
3	1,000	3,000	300
4	1,000	4,000	400
5	1,000	5,000	500
6	1,000	6,000	600
7	1,000	7,000	700
8	1,000	8,000	800
9	1,000	9,000	900
10	1,000	10,000	1,000
Total	$10,000	$10,000	$5,500

At the end of 10 years the total debt amounts to $10,000. The interest for just the last year is equal to the amount borrowed that year. Paying only the annual interest, the cost of their folly has amounted to $5,500 in the 10 years. And they still owe $10,000. That's costly!

Most people are aware of the scriptural principle that you reap what you sow. The crop reaped from debt is *interest*.

Freedom is lost. "Just as the rich rule the poor, so the borrower is servant to the lender" (Proverbs 22:7). The person in debt is in bondage to his creditors. A portion of his pay is committed to pay back the debt; choices as to how to spend his pay are lost. A share of his possessions is usually pledged to assure repayment; the sale of these pledged possessions is not possible without the creditor's permission. Such freedom is usually not granted unless the creditor is paid in full, a situation which is seldom possible from the proceeds of the sale of the mortgaged property.

Other freedoms are also involved. I've noticed that money that is borrowed with a smile is usually paid back with a scowl. Debt is often a thief of joy. But I've seen hundreds experience the relief and joy that comes when they've allowed God to lead them out of the debt trap. They've taken to heart God's message: "Evil men borrow and 'cannot pay it back'! But the good man returns what he owes with some extra besides" (Psalms 37:21).

You may have avoided the debt trap. Great! You can stay out of debt by design. A positive decision against borrowing money is the place to start. The chances are you've made other similar decisions for your life.

As a high-school student, I remember facing the decision about drinking. It seemed clear to me that I could decide either to drink alcoholic beverages or not to drink them. While a college freshman I studied all the books and periodicals in the library that I could find on the subject of alcohol. As a result of thoughtful study, I decided against drinking. I have never regretted that decision.

Your own decision to keep out of debt can provide a foundation for all of your financial planning. I've never talked with anyone who regretted his decision to avoid borrowing money.

If you are already in the debt trap, you must realize that you are in violation of God's commandment. You undoubtedly can testify to the cost of debt and the loss of freedoms. You may now be eager to find out how to escape the trap. Here's how a young man named Joe presented his situation to me.

Joe was in a fix! After hearing a message on faith, he had written checks for over $400 to pay his past-due bills. Next, he had boldly placed the checks in the mailbox. Then he prayed that God would honor his faith and fill his empty bank account with enough money to cover the checks.

This particular morning Joe had awakened with doubts in his mind. Had he acted first and prayed later? Would insufficient funds to cover the checks be a poor witness to his creditors? Was he putting God to a foolish test? Should he seek Christian counsel before it was too late? The young man called his pastor who referred him to me. As we talked in my office, the story of this new Christian's financial entanglement gradually unfolded.

Joe had invited Christ into his life just two months before. He was married and had a daughter aged two and a half. While attending the university, he operated a rural newspaper route. Since his marriage he and his wife had piled up total debts of $10,238. These included a mortgage on a mobile home, debt on his cars, and various other delinquent accounts. The major portion of his debt, however, was on the mobile home and cars.

Joe itemized his living expenses at $437 per month. He told me that his paper route netted him $490. It appeared that he had $53 left each month with which to meet additional expenses. If so, I pondered, why was he accumulating so much debt?

"Tell me about your paper route," I said.

He replied, "It's a rural route. I work three hours, both morning and afternoon, five days a week. On Saturday and Sunday I work three and one-half hours a day."

On paper I calculated that Joe was working 37 hours a week and, with 4⅓ weeks in a month, he was putting in a total of 160 hours. We also subtracted the $90 a month he was spending for automobile expenses from the $490 income from the paper route. We came up with an actual net of $400. After dividing 160 (hours worked per month) into the $400, I pointed out to him that he was earning $2.50 per hour.

But why was his debt accumulating so rapidly? We talked some more.

"How many miles do you drive on the route?" I asked.

"Well, the entire route is fifty miles," he answered.

"And you drive that twice a day?"

"That's right," he replied, "five days a week, and also once on Saturday and Sunday."

We found another sheet of paper and figured 600 miles per week times $4\frac{1}{3}$ weeks per month equaled 2,600 miles per month.

"How much do you think it costs to drive your car a mile?"

"Well," he said, "I've always heard that you can't drive a car for less than ten cents a mile."

"Okay, Joe, let's start with that."

We wrote: 2,600 miles $\times$ .10 = $260.00 per month, car expense.

"What is your total gross income from the newspapers?"

He replied, "My gross is five hundred ninety dollars, but my newspapers cost me seventy dollars and postage is another sixteen dollars per month."

His paper-route expenses looked like this: car, $260 + cost of papers, $70 + postage, $16 = $346 each month. Subtracting these expenses from the $590 gross income, we found he actually netted only $244. No wonder his debts were piling up! His income was really $193 *less* than his estimated monthly living expenses of $437.

I then took the pencil and divided 160 hours of work into the $244 net income from the route. He was shocked to find he netted only $1.52 per hour, or well under the current minimum wage. The fellow's response fascinated me.

Excitedly he asked, "Hey, I can't afford that job, can I?" Almost without hesitation he added, "Can *anybody* afford that job?"

I didn't need to answer his questions. The figures on paper made it obvious to both of us the real source of Joe's financial problems. Quickly I pointed out to my eager listener that any young man who could crawl out of bed in the middle of the night, drive fifty miles to deliver papers in all kinds of weather, then go back several afternoons and do the same thing, and still carry a full load at school, is the kind of person who is worth more than $1.52 per hour to most any em-

ployer. He readily agreed; an analysis of the facts had spoken clearly
to him.

Joe had been faked out. The Bible warns us: "Get the facts at any
price, and hold on tightly to all the good sense you can get" (Proverbs 23:23). The key to Joe's problems was to gather up the facts
about his earnings and his spending. With a new job that paid him
more nearly what he was worth—plus some valuable fringes such as
medical insurance—Joe was well on his way out of the debt trap.

Each journey out of the debt trap is different. Yet, each escape has
its own individual rewards and satisfactions. You may be fascinated
to discover the challenge involved in working your way out of the
bog and the mire of indebtedness.

2 Escaping the Debt Trap

Have you ever skied? Zooming down the slopes is exhilarating. Climbing up without a lift is a different story. You would not knowingly ski where the lifts were not functioning.

Zooming into debt is also exciting. However, the price of escaping from the trap is greater than most people realize. Simply to stop overspending is not enough. A *triple financial reverse* is involved. Look at these steps which must be taken in order to work out of the debt trap.

STOP SPENDING MORE THAN YOU MAKE!

REPAY THE DEBT!

PAY THE INTEREST!

Since our unsuspecting spender had been blowing $1,000 more each year than he made, his first step is to stop that practice. Changing his habit of overspending will not be easy. He may agree with the fellow who said that most of us would be delighted to pay as we go if we could just catch up with paying as we've gone!

But, if you think that's hard, visualize his efforts to eliminate the debt, without further borrowing; he must make payments on the principal *and* continue to pay interest. Figures in Table 3 reveal the hard road of payments ahead to eliminate the debt of $10,000 accumulated in 10 years of overspending. Assume the family paid off $1,000 each year on their debt—in addition to paying the interest.

What did it cost to accumulate $10,000 of debt over 10 years at a

Table 3: Cost of Debt Payment

Year	Payment	Interest	Balance Due $10,000
1	$ 2,000	$1,000	$9,000
2	1,900	900	8,000
3	1,800	800	7,000
4	1,700	700	6,000
5	1,600	600	5,000
6	1,500	500	4,000
7	1,400	400	3,000
8	1,300	300	2,000
9	1,200	200	1,000
10	1,100	100	. . . . .
Total	$15,500	$5,500	

10% interest rate? What was the interest cost during a repayment period of 10 years?

Interest first 10 years	$5,500
Interest last 10 years	$5,500
Total Interest	$11,000
Average annual interest 20 years	$550

What a price to pay for the temporary pleasure of overspending each paycheck! Do you see clearly what it means to work for your money? Do you understand why EASY PAYMENTS NOW make most people uneasy later?

The combination of change from overspending $1,000 per year to reducing expenses by $1,550 (in order to meet the average payment) is a $2,550 per year change in a living standard. Few people ever make the effort. In fiscal year 1975, 224,229 Americans resorted to personal bankruptcy rather than make the effort to repay their debts.

However, Jesus said, "What is impossible with men is possible with God" (see Luke 18:27 RSV). Escaping from the debt trap to the glory of God is a tremendous objective. Here are the steps to help you work out your own plan for escape.

1. Set a goal.
2. Start giving a set percentage of your income to the Lord.
3. List all you owe and all you own.
4. Have a sale.
5. Fix a monthly debt-payment amount.
6. Add no new debts.
7. Establish a time goal.
8. Cut the goal in half.
9. Develop a repayment schedule.
10. Share the repayment schedule with your creditors.
11. Stick to your plan.

Your journey to financial freedom must necessarily be an individual one. Your own circumstances will have a lot to say about your plan. The steps that are listed can serve as a guide to map out your own course. A brief explanation will help you understand its simplicity as well as its usefulness.

1. *Set a goal.*   One of my friends says he would rather aim at something and miss it than to aim at nothing and hit it. Deciding to get out of debt is the very first step.

Think for a minute about the benefits of getting out of debt. Such action will: reduce your expenses; delight your creditors; provide financial freedom; and please God. Such benefits provide excellent motivation for setting a goal of paying all your debts. Since a clear goal will put you out in front of 95 people out of every 100, you are well on your way to becoming debt-free. Incidentally, I've never seen anyone get out of debt by accident.

2. *Start giving a set percentage of your income to the Lord.*   Most Christians abandon their giving along the path into the debt trap. People reason that it does not make sense to give money away when there is not enough to pay the bills. God says, "But seek first his kingdom and his righteousness, and all these things shall be yours as well" (Matthew 6:33 RSV). In my opinion, *seeking first* means giving the first part of your income to the Lord.

Do you want God's blessing stamped on your get-out-of-debt project? Then don't be foolish and keep going into debt with God.

I've seen many try it, but no one succeeds. Start giving a set percentage of your income out of each paycheck.

3. *List all you owe and all you own.* It may be difficult to believe, but most people don't have a good grasp of what they owe. A listing of all your debts, with the monthly payment required and the annual percentage rate of interest, can be most helpful. The headings on the "What We Owe" list would look like this: Who We Owe; Total Amount Due; Monthly Payment; Interest Rate; and Percent of Total Debt.

Now list "What We Own." This list would include most of the things bought with borrowed money. Such items as automobiles, furniture, appliances, your home, and luxury objects might be some of what you own. (See Financial Summary, Chapter 7.)

Take a good look at both lists. Under "What We Owe" did you include any amounts due relatives? I find that people frequently neglect to put family loans on their lists, feeling that they don't have to be repaid. Put them on your list. They certainly are a part of what you owe.

Have you included everything you own—musical instruments, collections, guns, sports equipment, or hobbies?

4. *Have a sale.* Study the list of things you own. Which of these *can* you do without? Notice, I didn't say *want* to do without. Most people have no idea of what they can do without until they try. One couple who counseled with me recently discovered they could eliminate 20% of their total debt by selling one car. Then they were able to apply the amount of the car payment to further debt reduction. Don't think about how much you will lose of what you paid for the item you are selling. Think how much you will gain which can be applied to your debt reduction immediately.

Your attitude about things will determine your success in working your way out of the debt trap. I remember one young lady who came to me for counseling. Her finances were a mess. There were insufficient funds to cover a string of checks she had written. Her car payments were three months past due. Many charge accounts were delinquent. Creditors were after her constantly.

As we gathered the facts about her finances, I saw the difficulty of her continuing to make car payments and operate an automobile. "Could you get along without your car?" I asked her. Her reply was so quick that it surprised me. "Impossible!" she exclaimed.

With the knowledge of the following facts I failed to see the impossibility of her getting along without a car. She lived within easy walking distance of work, and bus transportation was very convenient. Furthermore, some neighbors and fellow employees had offered her rides to and from work and church. Also shopping was convenient to her house. With her attitude, it was really impossible to clear up her financial plight. Within a few weeks she had lost her job because of repercussions from her personal financial irresponsibility.

5. *Set a monthly debt-payment amount.* You will have to squeeze this money out of your monthly income. Now divide this figure into the total amount you owe to arrive at the number of months it will take you to be debt-free. Interest will add slightly to the time schedule, but the answer you get gives you the minimum amount of time for your debt-repayment plan.

6. *Add no new debts.* You must decide once and for all that you will not borrow money for any reason or charge any items. This would be an excellent time to have a credit-card-destruction ceremony in your home. Gather your family around, take a large pair of scissors, and deliberately cut each credit card into tiny pieces. Make a list of all charge accounts. Call or write each store and tell them to close your account. You cannot work your way out of debt if you continue to add new borrowings.

The key to your success in avoiding new debt will be to *do without*. You will be amazed at all of the so-called necessities you will learn to do without. One of my friends made all sorts of interesting discoveries during his journey out of debt. When the disposal broke, his family found that they could carry garbage out to the trash. When the dishwasher broke, they realized the joys of family fellowship while various members assisted Mother in doing the dishes. When the dryer went out, they discovered how fresh and clean clothes smell when hung outside to dry. You too will be in for some exciting revelations as you learn to do without.

7. *Establish a time goal.* Write down the number of months according to your plan that it will take to become debt-free.

8. *Cut the goal in half.* That's right! If you have determined that it will take you four years, or forty-eight months, to get out of debt, then write down a figure of one-half that time. You may think that I've gone crazy. But let me give you a simple formula for cutting your debt repayment time in half.

What is the amount of money you plan to set aside each month for debt payment? An examination of Table 4 will show you how long it will take you to pay off various amounts of debt with specific monthly-payment amounts. Assume the money was borrowed at an annual interest rate of 12%.

Table 4: Debt Pay-Off
(Interest Rate—12%)

Years to Pay Off Debt	1	1½	2	2½	3	4	5
Debt	Monthly Payments						
$ 1,000	$ 88.85	$ 60.99	$ 47.08	$ 38.75	$ 33.22	$ 26.34	$ 22.25
2,000	177.70	121.97	94.15	77.50	66.43	52.67	44.49
3,000	266.55	182.95	141.23	116.25	99.65	79.01	66.64
4,000	355.40	243.93	188.30	155.00	132.86	105.34	88.98
5,000	444.25	304.92	235.37	193.75	166.08	131.67	111.23
6,000	533.10	365.90	282.45	232.49	199.29	158.01	133.47
7,000	621.95	426.88	329.52	271.24	232.51	184.34	155.72
8,000	710.80	487.86	376.59	309.99	265.72	210.68	177.96
9,000	799.64	548.84	423.67	348.74	298.93	237.01	200.21
10,000	888.49	609.83	470.74	387.49	332.15	263.34	222.45
12,000	1,066.19	731.79	564.89	464.98	398.58	316.01	266.94
14,000	1,243.89	853.75	659.03	542.48	465.01	368.68	311.43
16,000	1,421.59	975.72	753.18	619.97	531.43	421.35	355.92

Assume you have set aside $111.23 monthly to repay your debt of $5,000. It will take you 5 years of monthly payments to pay off this debt. Remember I said that you should cut your time schedule in half. Look down the chart at the $5,000 to find the amount of monthly payment it takes to pay off your debt in 2½ years. The figure is $193.75. Paying your debt in 2½ years (30 months) at $193.75 monthly costs you a total of $5,812.50. Taking 5 years (60 months) to pay the same $5,000 back at $111.23 a month costs you a total of $6,673.80. That's $861.30 more in interest costs and that should give you sufficient incentive to look hard at my plan for cutting your debt-payment time in half.

Here's how you can do it. Subtract the $111.23 monthly payment from the $193.75 monthly payment. Your additional monthly cost to pay off your debt in half the time is not twice $111.23—but only $82.52. The only way I know to save money in paying off debts is to pay them off faster. The faster you pay, the less it costs.

"But," you ask, "how can we come up with $82.52 a month above our payment of $111.23? Haven't we pared our budget to the bare bone?" You probably have. Your solution to the problem will depend upon your family's creativity.

Again, let's look at the objective. The challenge is to cut your debt-repayment time in half. Expressing this goal in positive terms would be to say that you are going to get out of debt twice as fast as you had planned. Certainly to do that you don't have to double your income or cut your expenses in half. In the illustration we've used, you only need $82.52 more each month to pay on your debt.

Let me challenge your thinking as to how to do that. At the moment unemployment in the United States is at the highest level since the depression of the 1930s. In great contrast, however, there are many opportunities for income that go begging because no one can be found to do the work. For example, consider domestic help. Yes, that's what I mean—housecleaning. Domestic help now comes under the Federal Minimum-Wage Law. The hourly rate is a minimum of $2.30 —that's $18.40 for an 8-hour day. Maybe you don't want your wife to work. However, the possibility of her working one day or two mornings per week cleaning someone else's house could bring in approximately $80 per month (before taxes).

Another alternative would be to have the whole family clean a house on Saturdays. You could surely find a family in your neighborhood who wants their house cleaned and who would be willing to pay your whole family to do the job at a family hourly rate. Investing every Saturday to cut your debt-repayment time in half would be a worthwhile family project.

Remember the old joke about the magazine salesman who knocked on your door with the opening statement, "I'm working my way through college"? Maybe your family slogan could be, "We're working our way out of debt."

Other family projects might involve baby-sitting or working for temporary campaigns such as health foundations, fund drives, or political campaigns. Many churches have difficulty finding volunteer help and are willing to pay for part-time jobs in the kitchen, in the church nurseries, or even part-time custodial help. To add $82 to your monthly income takes only $18.92 per week. At the $2.30 minimum wage, that is only 8 to 9 hours of work per week. With two family members working, such as on a Saturday morning or Saturday evening or even one night a week, it would only take four hours of work a week.

Can you visualize a regular weekly project of working this amount of time together as a way of cutting down $2\frac{1}{2}$ years of debt payments? If you have teen-age youngsters, then allowing them to have a part in the debt-repayment program could be excellent training.

How can you find a place to sell your services to add extra income to move you out of the debt trap more quickly? People say they can't find anyone to do certain jobs these days. What are these jobs? Try to find out; ask people. I've had a man and his wife clean my office for 21 years; they have done this three nights a week after his regular work. This is when they get in all their talk time. Finding dependable janitorial service is often a problem for small-business offices that require cleaning only once or twice a week. Most often the small business will furnish the necessary equipment. Inquire of churches in your neighborhood; ask questions at the stores where you shop; ask around where you work. Keep your eyes open for lawns that need mowing or shrubs that need trimming, right in your own neighborhood. You'll be surprised how much you're worth if you're only willing to invest a few hours a week.

Imaginative ways to earn extra money are limited only by a lack of creativity and desire. Here are just a few ideas to stimulate your thinking:

ushering at concerts, sporting events
walking pets
pet-sitting while owners are gone
tutoring children in schoolwork
typing term papers
house-sitting, including plant care, security checks
shoveling snow
raking leaves, yard work
stripping wallpaper
window washing, car washing
painting, inside and out
cooking and cleanup when others entertain in their home

Another way to hasten your escape from the debt trap is to agree in advance to add any extra income to debt repayment. This would include raises, bonuses, tax refunds, garage sale income, or any other unusual income that comes into your family.

9. *Develop a repayment schedule.* Usually writing down your plan will help you to achieve it. Use notebook paper and allow enough space to include the number of months to fulfill your plan. The chart would look like this:

Repayment Schedule	January	February	March	April
Creditor A				
Payment Planned				
Amount Paid				
Balance Due				

Continue with a listing of each creditor in the left column and add to the months according to your plan. Be sure to total the payments and the balance due.

Take the amount you owe off of the list you've made; divide it by the number of months you plan to take to get out of debt. Insert that figure under Payment Planned. At the end of each month, after you've made your payments, write down the amount paid and the balance due. You can also keep a monthly total of the payments to all creditors and the balance due on all your debts at the end of each month. Recording your payments will give you a sense of satisfaction. Watching the balances diminish will give you an excitement that will help you stick to your goal.

10. *Take or send a copy of your repayment schedule to your creditors.* I promise you that they will be very impressed with the fact that you have made out a plan. They will be even more impressed as you send them the regular monthly payment you have promised. Also tell them that if something happens to delay their payment, you will contact them ahead of the date when the payment is due.

I have worked with hundreds of credit grantors. I have yet to find one who will not go along with a person who makes an honest effort to pay some amount regularly on his bill. It is rare to find a creditor who will turn an account over to a collection agency when the debtor has communicated in advance of missing a promised payment.

11. *Stick to your plan.* You'll be tempted again and again to quit. Don't do it! Each missed payment will set you back on your goal. Ideas such as: *It won't hurt to miss the debt payment this month, after all, it's December!* or *Why bother to keep all those records?* are simple tools of the Devil which keep you from escaping the debt trap to the glory of God.

Starting something is easier than finishing. More start the race than finish. Life is littered with dropouts who quit when the going gets rough. The Bible has a very specific word of encouragement as you escape the debt trap: "Having started the ball rolling so enthusiastically, you should carry this project through to completion just as gladly, giving whatever you can out of whatever you have. Let your enthusiastic idea at the start be equalled by your realistic action now" (2 Corinthians 8:11).

Escaping the debt trap will require persistence. Some new attitudes about your way of living will be essential. Huffing and puffing with your money must be replaced by a different way of financial breathing—living on a margin.

3 Living on a Margin

Do you arrive at places on time?

Are you usually early?

Are you frequently late?

If your experience is similar to mine, you find that it is difficult, if not impossible, for most of us to arrive at places exactly on time. We are usually early or late. Our habits are well established; the early bird is consistent, and the late-arrivers are regularly late.

I did some thinking about my own pattern of going places. In all honesty I can say that my usual arrival at appointments averaged five minutes past the starting time. Look at how this affected me during the past sixteen years.

```
    365  days
   ×16   years
  5,840  days in 16 years
    ×3   estimated number of appointments per day
 17,520  total appointments
    ×5   minutes late on the average
 87,600  total minutes late
  1,460  total hours late
     61  total days late
      2  months late
```

You may be astounded to see, as I was, that during the past sixteen years my five minutes of being late have added up to two full months of twenty-four-hour days.

In thinking about arriving late, I realized that the two months of late minutes were greatly overshadowed by the fact that, for each time I was five minutes late, I spent about fifteen minutes *hurrying to be late.*

I believe a person should take care of his body. That's just good stewardship. Consequently, each week I try to swim, jog, or ride a bicycle at least five times. This works off accumulated tensions and helps keep my body in physical condition. The medical experts tell me exercise is a great preventive when it comes to heart attacks.

Everything I read about the heart states tension is one of the leading killers. What a revelation! During the past sixteen years, I had spent an additional six months of twenty-four-hour days pushing, rushing, pressing, and straining while hurrying to arrive five minutes late. It also seemed true in my case that, when hurrying to be late, circumstances often occurred which put me under additional pressures and caused me to be even later—and certainly more tense.

Another observation is that after I had arrived someplace late, I was angry with myself, self-centered, and seldom mentally prepared to participate in the situation for which I had hurried to be late.

In a radio program titled "Start Late, Stay Late," Earl Nightingale summed it up this way, "When you start late, it seems that all the forces on earth conspire to further delay you." If you start late, you just never catch up. Nightingale continues, "One of the most important lessons a person can learn, in my opinion, is to start early. It can probably even add years to his life span. When you start early, everything goes great, nothing ever seems to go wrong and the whole day is better for it. You're relaxed, smiling and comfortable."

While pondering my own bad habits in this area, I had lunch with a man who is an elder in our church. As I drove downtown to pick him up—late of course—the thought struck me that John was always early for appointments. I had confidence that he would be on the corner earlier than the time we had set. When he got into the car, I asked him, "John, how do you manage to arrive every place early?"

He replied with a question to me, "When do *you* plan to arrive?" My answer was that I tried to be there just on time. "That's your problem," John said, "you've got to operate on a margin and plan to get there early."

Instantly I learned a valuable lesson. I started allowing at least a five-to-ten-minute margin in my time plans. Going places now is almost like being on vacation. There is time to observe the sights, hear the sounds, smell the smells, and still arrive in a relaxed manner. Living on a *time margin* has done wonders for my health and my attitude. Earl Nightingale was right; so was John.

Living on a *financial margin* has attractive benefits too. Since there are only three ways to handle your income, you have a choice. You can save money, which is operating on a financial margin. You can break even, which is spending exactly what you make. Or, you can go into debt, which is spending more than you make. Plunging into debt, while overspending a $12,000 income by $1,000 annually is arriving 5 minutes late with your money.

Solomon tells us, "The wise man saves for the future, but the foolish man spends whatever he gets" (Proverbs 21:20). Saving money makes us wise in God's sight. Furthermore, saving money produces exciting economic rewards. Assuming an income of $12,000 per year, a 5-minute margin would amount to 8.3% of the income, or approximately $1,000 per year. Let's see what happens with the family that saves 8.3% of a $12,000 income and receives 6% interest, compounded annually, for 10 years. Table 5 on page 36 shows the advantages of the financial margin.

Are you amazed to see that $10,000 saved has increased to $13,972 because of compound interest? By saving $1,000 at 6% interest during each of 10 years you are able to withdraw $2,000 per year for 8 years, or a total of $16,000, and still have $1,286 left in your account.

Can you grasp the staggering differences between saving the equivalent of 5 minutes of your money versus living about 5 minutes late with your income? The dollar differences are amazing. The 5-minute margin results in interest additions to your money of $3,972. The example discussed in Chapter 1 showed a borrower who was 5 minutes late with his income and borrowed at 10% interest charges. This cost him $5,500 and he still had the 10-year accumulated debt to repay.

While withdrawing your savings over the succeeding years, you will earn an additional $3,314 in interest. During the period of planned savings and withdrawal your savings will earn a total of $7,286 in-

Table 5: The Financial Margin

Growth of Savings
(Interest 6%)

Year	Amount	Interest Earned	Ending Balance
1	$ 1,000	$ 60.00	$ 1,060.00
2	1,000	123.60	2,183.60
3	1,000	191.02	3,374.62
4	1,000	262.48	4,637.10
5	1,000	338.23	5,975.33
6	1,000	418.52	7,393.85
7	1,000	503.63	8,897.48
8	1,000	593.85	10,491.33
9	1,000	689.48	12,180.81
10	1,000	790.85	13,971.66
Total	$10,000	$3,971.66	

Planned Withdrawals

Year	Amount	Interest Earned	Ending Balance
11	$ 2,000	$ 718.30	$12,689.96
12	2,000	641.40	11,331.36
13	2,000	559.88	9,891.24
14	2,000	473.47	8,364.71
15	2,000	381.88	6,746.59
16	2,000	284.80	5,031.39
17	2,000	181.88	3,213.27
18	2,000	72.80	1,286.07
19	1,286	. . . . . .	. . . .
Total	$17,286	$3,314.41	

terest. For the period of debt accumulation *and* repayment the interest costs were $11,000. (*See* Chapter 2.) There is a whopping $18,286 difference between living on a margin with your money versus choosing the debt-trap way.

There are two types of people: those who work for their money, and those who have their money work for them. Which type would you choose to be?

God commends the ant for its wisdom in following the savings principle: "There are . . . things that are small but unusually wise: Ants aren't strong, but store up food for the winter . . ." (*see* Proverbs 30:24).

You may see the wisdom of living on a financial margin and saving money. But you don't see how you can save in your present situation. The Scriptures never tell us to do anything without giving us some direction in accomplishing the task. There is a very clear principle in the Bible that could possibly revitalize your entire financial situation. It is the principle of *contentment*.

BLONDIE®

© King Features Syndicate 1975.

4 Be Content With What You Have

Have you ever referred to those huge catalogues as "wish books"? *I wish* summarizes the state where most people live—the state of discontentment.

The dictionary defines *discontent* as a dislike of what one has and a desire for something different; feeling not satisfied; uneasiness; restlessness. As I ponder this definition, I think of so many people whose lives are characterized by discontent. They fill their bedrooms with king-size beds and their houses with everything imaginable. They then feel crowded; and they either build an addition onto their house or buy a bigger one. Meanwhile, the process of buying more "stuff" continues.

An unknown skeptic has summarized financial discontent in this way: "People buy things they don't need, with money they don't have, to impress neighbors they don't even like!"

If you live now, or have ever lived, in the state of discontentment, you know that one word describes it all—*misery*. The cycle of wanting, shopping, buying, and filling doesn't add up. The total comes to an empty bank account plus an insatiable desire for still more stuff!

Shirley Rice, a Christian wife and mother, has had a great ministry in our home with her taped series and her booklet *The Christian Home, A Woman's View*. (Norfolk, Virginia: The Tabernacle Church of Norfolk, 1965.) In her chapter on "The Atmosphere of the Home" she gives feminine insights on women's attitudes toward "things":

We haven't learned to "sit loose to the world and everything in it" as Matthew Henry says. "Whatever you have of the world in your hands, keep it out of your heart." We set great store by "things"; we are never satisfied with what we have. We push our husbands to get ahead; we covet this and that. Never being satisfied makes us tense. Proverbs 15:27 says "He that is greedy of gain troubleth his own house." David said in Psalms 131:2, "I have behaved myself as a weaned child." [See KJV.] Are we weaned from our desires for things of a material nature? Covetousness begins when we cannot be content with what we have. It is not that you do not need a new rug, nor is it that it is wrong for you to have it; but the sin is that you cannot be content with what you have until such time as you can afford the new one.

The Bible clearly establishes God's principle of contentment: "Keep your life free from love of money, and be content with what you have; for he has said, 'I will never fail you nor forsake you' " (Hebrews 13:5 RSV).

You may have already noticed that contentment does not depend upon what you have. Paul defines contented living, showing how our attitudes are the real key: "Our hearts ache, but at the same time we have the joy of the Lord. We are poor, but we give rich spiritual gifts to others. We own nothing, and yet we enjoy everything" (2 Corinthians 6:10).

Enjoyment and contentment do not depend upon ownership. We would enjoy very little if ownership was the requirement.

I have had a pilot's license since 1963. I can't imagine that anyone enjoys flying a small plane any more than I do. I've literally covered the United States by plane, exhilarated by the unique challenges of each trip. But I have never owned an airplane. For the amount of flying I do, it would cost me over $2,000 a year to own a plane instead of renting one.

Years ago I calculated that my two daughters would probably choose to go to college. The dubious benefits of airplane ownership, when compared to the plan to have college funds set aside by the time of their high-school graduation, motivated me to continue renting.

There were hassles in renting. I didn't always make every trip I planned. However, there were enough trips to log over 100,000 miles. When time for college arrived, there was enough money set aside to pay the expenses.

The ownership of luxury items seldom makes sound financial sense. Campers, boats, cabins, and airplanes are all items that are costly to buy and to maintain. Their upkeep also takes time—time that could be used for the Lord's work.

Bill Gothard, who is President of the Institute in Basic Youth Conflicts, Oak Brook, Illinois, defines *contentment* as: "realizing that God has provided everything I need for my present circumstances." The man who is satisfied with little has everything. If you haven't got what you like, like what you have.

God revealed a very powerful principle to me early one morning while I was kneeling in prayer at our couch in the family room. The regular use of this prayer principle has the potential for eliminating discontentment. The principle is that of *giving thanks* to God in prayer.

As I prayed, I was overwhelmed with thanksgiving to God for my wife and her spirit of contentment. I thanked Him quickly that she was still contented with the furniture in our family room. We had bought the couch from a neighbor fifteen years earlier at a price of fifty dollars. Another couch, chair, and tables were hand-me-downs from Marjean's parents. Nineteen years ago we had refinished these things when the girls were babies. The breakfast table and chairs had been bought for thirty-four dollars in a junk shop and had been antiqued. I thought about all the men I know whose wives are constantly nagging them for newer stuff. Then I thanked Him again for a contented wife. I remembered that my two daughters had been content to grow up with no color-television set and had driven old cars. I thanked Him for Jenny's and Amy's attitudes of contentment.

God's Word summarizes this principle in Psalms: "It is good to say, 'Thank you' to the Lord, to sing praises to the God who is above all gods. Every morning tell him, 'Thank you for your kindness,' and every evening rejoice in all his faithfulness" (Psalms 92:1, 2).

A simple jingle has helped us evaluate possible purchases in our home. You might measure all prospective purchases against its standards:

> Use it up,
> Wear it out,
> Make it do,
> Do without.

Recently I saw a sign that has kept me from many purchases: YOU HAVE NO IDEA OF THE THINGS YOU CAN DO WITHOUT—UNTIL YOU TRY. One January our family made a list of items we wanted to buy during the year. We agreed to not consider actually purchasing them until the middle of the year. In July, when we looked at the list, we were glad we hadn't bought some of the items; *we no longer wanted them!*

The world has some tremendous advertising tools that aim to create dissatisfaction in our lives. These devices are potent and very effective. Three powerful weapons of the advertising world bear examination so we can avoid their influence in our lives.

Television   One of my friends calls the TV set a "moron-o-scope." But those who create the commercials are far from morons. Their brainchildren are programmed to keep you from being content with what you have. Have you ever noticed that the one-half hour of evening news, weather, and sports usually has thirteen commercials which make up one-fourth of the thirty minutes? Surveys show that Americans sometimes average over six hours per day viewing television. During this time there are over a hundred commercials planned to motivate you to buy or to do something. Is it any wonder that contentment vanishes and wants increase in proportion to the amount of TV-viewing time?

To bring the TV set into focus as an influential factor, consider these facts. Between the key developmental ages of three and eighteen, the average American is spending twenty-two thousand hours watching television. The same average American, if he is a better-than-average churchgoer, will spend at the most three thousand hours in church and Sunday school. Which influence will have the greater impact?

A Hesston, Kansas, family has never owned a television set. Their six children have grown up without the benefit of this modern electronic wonder. If you shared the hospitality of their home, as we have been privileged to do on many occasions, you would be thrilled with the courtesy, the family spirit, and the contentment that were apparent. Obviously, there's been more involved than the absence of a television set. But they have taken their stand; they are a family of participants—in music, sports, and family duties—instead of a household of spectators.

Shopping One Wichita physician had a very interesting rule for his wife. She was directed to order all her groceries over the phone at one of a handful of stores which would deliver those groceries to his home. When she ordered by phone, he knew that she had to work from a list. In order to control the grocery bill, he didn't want his wife exposed to the techniques of the hidden persuaders who lay out and develop our supermarkets in such a way as to encourage us to buy more than we need. Although the prices were higher where she phoned, he figured he could afford to pay more on the items ordered compared to the impulse purchases his wife would make if she went into the store.

This is an extreme illustration; but most of us have learned that the more shopping we do, the more we spend. My wife proved this when she went on several shopping trips with our oldest daughter, Jenny, prior to her leaving for college. For the first time in many months I found Marjean's wants increasing beyond her clothing budget. Out in stores she found many "bargains" and "cute things" that she felt she could not live without. Fortunately, the reality of a budget kept her from overspending. Marjean has also learned not to send me by the store on my way home from work. Hungry husbands make poor shoppers.

When we were expecting our first child, a door-to-door saleswoman appeared with an offer for a long-term subscription to *Parents Magazine* and a large, "free" medical book. Marjean promptly signed on the dotted line and wrote out her check, feeling pleased with herself.

A few minutes later she began to think about how she would explain the "good deal" to me. Was it really a deal? Would I be mad? Had she paid too much? She wanted to back out. She raced out the door and found the saleswoman up at the end of the block. Would you believe that the woman said she had already put the order in the mailbox?

When I came home from work, Marjean told me the story. She had
subscribed to the magazine for several years. Even then, the price per
issue was above the newsstand price. A quick check of the Sears
Catalogue showed reduced prices per issue available for shorter-
term subscriptions. Our so-called free medical book was not free at
all. We also learned that the Sears Catalogue can be a good counsel
for comparative shopping.

Newspapers, magazines, and catalogues   Advertising is calculated to
get you, the viewer, to buy. Spending time looking at ads is an excellent way to lose your contentment with what you have. Some
people have even gone so far as to cancel their magazine subscriptions and ask that their names be removed from catalogue lists. Within
the last thirty days I have received twelve catalogues containing over
two thousand pages of colorful, tempting merchandise.

Avoiding these enticements of television, shopping, magazines, and
catalogues can be a great aid in controlling your contentment.

God didn't command us to be content so that He could make us
miserable. Sowing discontent is what reaps misery.

The fruit of contentment is abundant. Joy, peace, and a thankful
spirit are three of these fruits. One of Paul's most exciting passages,
and certainly one of his most challenging, is in Philippians: "Not
that I was ever in need, for I have learned how to get along happily
whether I have much or little. I know how to live on almost nothing
or with everything. I have learned the secret of contentment in every
situation, whether it be a full stomach or hunger, plenty or want"
(Philippians 4:11, 12). Note that this is followed in verse 13 by Paul
confidently saying, ". . . I can do everything God asks me to with
the help of Christ who gives me the strength and power."

God is the secret of contentment!

5 The Old Clunker

The automobile is one item that keeps many families in a financial pinch. How easy it is to become discontented with your present car and succumb to the fever to trade for a newer model. New-car fever can't be cured with an aspirin, but it may be cooled by looking at some cold, hard facts about car costs.

Automobiles are seldom worn out when they are traded for later models. The proof of this is the fact that someone will buy your trade-in (probably for several hundred dollars more than you received for it), expecting to drive it many thousands of miles. Consider the reasons usually given for trading in a car: age, mileage, and needed repairs.

Age is no reason to trade in a car. My mother's car is now over 13 years old, but it still has less than 40,000 miles on it. Having spent most all of its nondriving time in a garage, the condition of its body is better than that of most cars half its age. While some cars are old after one year, a car can be relatively new after several years if it has had excellent care.

A recent experience dramatically illustrated that the age of a car is no reason for trading it. I serve communion monthly to a couple who are 85 and 86 years old. When I arrived one Sunday the woman was out in the garage. There I saw the car that they had bought in 1940—a 1940 Master Deluxe Chevrolet. It has been driven a total of 57,000 miles, and the engine has never had any major repairs. The car is still providing useful transportation for these folks.

That the car is still powerful was proven when the lady went to back the car out of the garage. Unintentionally she left the car in low gear instead of reverse. After the car was started, she released the clutch, and the car shot straight forward, removing the back of the garage in one big piece. Not one dent or scratch was on the front of the car, even though the entire back of the garage had been moved about ten feet forward into the backyard.

When the couple drives the car, they find people oohing and aahing over it. They have even had people follow them home and ask about buying the car. Would you advise these folks to trade for a newer model just because their car is 36 years old?

Age is not necessarily a reason to trade a car.

Mileage is usually not sufficient justification to trade in cars. The chairman of our deacons is a mechanic. He tells me that with proper maintenance and repairs most cars can be expected to perform satisfactorily up to 150,000 miles or more. A survey that I made at one automobile dealership revealed that, during a recent 3-month period, the average number of miles on the cars that were traded in was 60,285 miles. Of a substantial number of cars only 4 had mileage in excess of 100,000; the highest mileage on any trade-in was 112,112 miles. That's hardly driving your car to a successful conclusion. These facts support the proposition that most people trade in when their cars still have over half of their useful life remaining.

Repairs Buying a new car because your present car needs repairs seems almost as absurd as committing suicide because you need surgery.

A youth director was sent to me by her father for counsel about her car. Her present vehicle had under 100,000 miles on it, was less than 10 years old, but was suddenly in need of about $200 worth of repairs. Her father thought she should not waste any more money repairing the old clunker but should buy a new one. As we studied the facts of the two alternatives, we clearly saw that the economics favored fixing up the car she had.

You can seldom justify on a financial basis the purchase of a new car to replace one that needs repairs. An analysis of our own family auto reveals the difference in annual costs between buying a new car and keeping the old clunker. I have used for comparison the 1963 Chevy Impala that my wife drives and a 1976 Chevy with similar equipment. Comparative figures are shown in Table 6 on page 48.

This is an extreme example of comparing the cost of owning a thirteen-year-old car for three more years with buying a new car and its cost for the first three years. Figures for your own situation may be worked out by applying them to the same format. Check with your car dealer, bank or credit union, and insurance agent to assemble your facts. The facts usually prove that in almost every case it costs more to own and operate a newer car than an older one.

The principle in Scripture is that of gathering facts before making major purchases. God calls fact-finders *wise men:* "The wise man looks ahead. The fool attempts to fool himself and won't face facts" (Proverbs 14:8).

Facing facts is one very effective way to purge the urge to splurge. A little splurge here and there is most often the disaster that keeps you from making ends meet in your finances.

Your present car may be completely shot. An analysis of the facts may reveal to you that the purchase of a brand new auto is not within your means or your desire. Should you buy a used car? Why take on somebody else's problems? Where do you ever find a clean used car?

My recommendation would be to follow the plan of a young couple who are involved in a college ministry. The used car they had purchased several years before had over 140,000 miles on it. The body was badly rusted; the car had no air conditioning. They had reasons to begin looking for a newer model. They were expecting their first child in a few weeks. It would certainly be more pleasant to have an air-conditioned car for the wife and baby during the approaching hot summer. Their ministry also required them to take trips of some distance with students to various conferences during the summer.

Their requirements for an automobile were well thought out. They had been searching for the past six months for a three-year-old car, preferably a Ford, Chevrolet, or Plymouth four-door with an air conditioner, having less than thirty thousand miles on it, in excellent condition, and at a price of less than two thousand dollars.

Around the luncheon table in their home we all prayed together that God would supply a car to meet their specific requirements. Two days later I was back in Wichita talking to my neighbor. For the first time since we had prayed, I thought about my friends' need and our prayer. I asked my neighbor, "Would you happen to know anyone who has a three-year-old Ford, Chevrolet, or Plymouth, air-conditioned, four-door, with under thirty thousand miles that he wants to sell for about two thousand dollars?" His reply took me by complete surprise.

Table 6: Car Cost Comparison

1976 Chevy Impala, 4-Door Sedan
Air Conditioning, Power Steering, Automatic Transmission

Cost of New Car	
Price	$5,759.85
Less Trade-in, 1963 Chevy	−759.85
Net Cost	$5,000.00
Sales Tax	150.00
Total Cost	$5,150.00
Cash Down Payment	−450.00
Finance Amount	$4,700.00
Cost of Financing, 3 Years	
Car Note	$4,700.00
Credit Life Insurance	131.30
Interest	954.66
Total Note Due	$5,785.96
Monthly Payments	$ 160.72
Average Annual Cost, New Car	
Interest Charges	$ 318.00
Credit Life Insurance	44.00
Tax (3-year average)	141.00
Depreciation	950.00
Insurance	235.00
Total Annual Cost	$1,688.00

Table 6: Car Cost Comparison (cont.)

1963 Chevy, Value $150.00

Average Annual Cost, Old Car

Tax	$ 7.00
Depreciation	30.00
Insurance	133.00
Total Annual Cost	$ 170.00

Comparison of Ownership Costs, Annual

1976 Chevy	$1,688.00
1963 Chevy	170.00
Difference in Cost	$1,518.00
Assume Repairs to 1963 Car	500.00
Annual Savings	$1,018.00

Comparison of Mileage Costs: Cents per Mile

Miles per Year	1963 Chevy	1976 Chevy
5,000	13.4	33.8
10,000	6.7	16.9
15,000	4.5	11.3
20,000	3.4	8.4

"I sure do," he said; "it's a three-year-old Chevrolet Impala four-door." He gave me the name of a man whose wife had recently won a new car. They had just decided to sell the family automobile and keep the newer car.

Excitedly I called the man, a local realtor. As he described the car over the phone, I felt sure it was God's answer to prayer. Within a short time I had looked at the car and found that it met all of the requirements. I called the couple, and we agreed to put a deposit on the car until they could come and see it themselves. When they arrived and looked at the car, we all knew that God had specifically answered another prayer.

For two years Marjean and I prayed for God to supply a college for our daughter Jenny. Her needs seemed simple enough: a dynamic Christian school; a degree offered in physical education; and a girls' gymnastic program competing on a national level. Mom and Dad also had in mind a location within a 700-mile radius of Wichita—just right for weekend visits in a small airplane. We prayed and waited. We wrote over fifty letters and waited. We visited more than a dozen schools and waited. We attended two National NCAA Collegiate Gymnastic meets and still waited. High school graduation was less than eleven weeks away; we were all still praying and waiting.

One morning when I arrived at my office desk, I saw an alumni newspaper from Seattle Pacific College. Bob, a prayer partner of ten years, had left the paper there—open to a picture of SPC's new women's gym facility. A quick letter of inquiry to SPC brought this response about the girls' gymnastic program from the Athletic Director: ". . . we will undoubtedly step from relative obscurity to national prominence next year." Not only was the school Christian, but so were the coach and the leading performers of the team.

Were we to doubt God's provision for Jenny's needs, even though the school was three times farther away than we had hoped?

Much of the excitement of prayer involves our waiting for God's answers. Praying for financial needs usually means learning to wait expectantly for God's supply. His way often has exciting and unexpected solutions.

6 The Fallacy of the Working Mother

Tight family finances frequently trigger the decision for a wife to go to work. The U.S. Labor Department states that in 1974 over 31% of mothers with children under the age of three were employed. Why do mothers work? How do they fare financially?

Most working women have jobs so they can have "more money." Some have specific goals. A few of the goals that have been shared with me as I interviewed prospective employees are: to buy a camper, to buy a bigger house, to pay for a child's college education, or money to travel on vacations. Few ever tell me that they really want to work. One young lady recently shared her reasons for working— "I like money."

If almost one-third of the mothers of small children work, and if most of these work in order to increase income, then the jobs must be very lucrative.

Right?

Wrong!

I have even seen cases in which the costs of the mother's working exceeded her income; and, a net income of 20¢ to 40¢ an hour is the rule rather than the exception for a working mother.

Examine the figures for a mother who is earning $2.50 per hour and working a 40-hour week. The list is designed so that you can analyze your specific situation. My own experience indicates that

Income and Expenses of Working Mother

	Hypothetical		Yours
Gross Income Per Week		$100.00	_____
Less: Tithe	$10.00		_____
Paycheck Deductions:			
Federal Income Tax (20%)	20.00		_____
State Income Tax (10% of Federal)	2.00		_____
Social Security Tax	5.85		_____
Job-Related Expenses			
Transportation (10 trips of 5 miles @ 12¢)	6.00		_____
Child Care (1 child)	20.00		_____
Meals at Work, Coffee Breaks	6.00		_____
Eating Out and Convenience Foods	6.00		_____
Extra Clothes	6.00		_____
Beauty Shop	5.00		_____
Other "Bought-It-With-My-Money" Expenses	5.00		_____
Total Expenses	$91.85	91.85	_____
Net Addition to Family Income		$ 8.15	_____

these figures are pretty realistic. Some women maintain that they don't eat out or carry out food just because they are working. Others don't go to the beauty shop. But we haven't included those pesky "office collections," showers for the girls at work, or other probable expenses. Nor have we allowed for decreased income from days not worked because of sick children or emergencies at home.

Rarely will an employed mother net over $10 to $20 per week from her full-time job, if the financial facts of her employment are realistically faced. How much is she actually earning per hour?

On job per week	40 hours
Lunch hours away from home	5
Travel to and from job and sitter	5
Total hours away from home	50 hours
Net addition	$10–$20
Net additions per hour	20¢–40¢

Does a mother's earnings of 20¢–40¢ per hour from a full-time job enable her to measure up to the wife described in Proverbs? "If you can find a truly good wife, she is worth more than precious gems!" (Proverbs 31:10). The 20¢–40¢ per hour net hardly sounds like precious gems!

Some other characteristics of the godly woman described in Proverbs 31 include such activities as these:

> richly satisfying her husband's needs
> helping her husband
> preparing breakfast for her household
> watching for bargains
> sewing for her family
> sewing for the poor

How could a wife away from home 50 hours a week be expected to fulfill such responsibilities?

How then can a mother supplement the family income and still have time to manage the home? The answer is found in the wife's staying home and applying herself to certain tasks for 2 hours a day. Following are some examples of ways to save that $2.00 per day that 50 hours away from home adds to the family income of the working mother. Let's start with food.

Do you eat donuts? A dozen from the donut shop presently costs $2.05. Marjean makes 15 donuts from a tube of biscuits (21¢), ½ cup of sugar (11¢), a teaspoon of cinnamon (1¢), and 1¾ cup of oil for frying (84¢, but halved to 42¢ because she uses it over and over). This adds up to a total cost of 75¢. That works out to 60¢ per dozen, or a savings of $1.45 compared to the store-bought donuts. If you eat a dozen and a half a month, you've saved a *day's net earnings* by making your own.

Low-fat milk purchased at the store costs $1.44 per gallon. A national brand of instant non-fat dry milk which you mix yourself costs 80¢ a gallon. If you drink 3 gallons a week, the savings amounts to $1.92, or approximately the net you could add to the family earnings from a 10-hour day of working away from home.

Ways to save money at home by a wife "working" as a comparative shopper, a creative cook with planned menus, and a seamstress

Harried Harriet arrives exhausted from the hassles of the office and hastily whips up a late dinner before cleaning up the house, throwing a load of clothes in the washer, and finally collapsing into bed.

doing simple alterations and clothing repairs are practically unlimited. The net earnings at home, for only 2 hours of "home work" a day, would be at least $1.00 per hour—or 5 times the net earnings per hour of a full-time job. A mere 2 hours set aside each day for "home work" could easily replace that full-time job.

A weekly plan for 2 hours of "home work" daily might resemble this schedule:

Monday	baking
Tuesday	sewing
Wednesday	making gifts
Thursday	grocery shopping
Friday	casserole preparation, canning

The other eight hours each day are available for concentration on her role as a helpmate for her husband.

Peppy Peggy greets her husband at the door, bathed and smelling of fresh perfume. Dinner is ready and includes a hot loaf of his favorite bread with a jar of last summer's homemade strawberry preserves. After dinner his wife is available to him and the children, having completed her "home work."

Which do you think a husband prefers to see upon arriving home in the evening? Which woman has the best chance of cheerfully serving the Lord? Which woman has the best opportunity to balance the family budget? Which woman will likely have the calm and gentle spirit? And under which circumstances will the children have the best prospects of being brought up "in the discipline and instruction of the Lord"? (*See* Ephesians 6:4 RSV.)

7 Budgeting—What Is It?

Budgeting is planned spending! Doesn't that sound easy?

And budgeting *is* easy when you understand its purpose, follow a workable system, and use it to maximize the family income. A family that knows where its money is going can usually make it go farther.

Most of the money you earn in your life, you will spend. You will spend your funds for things you want. Unfortunately, your yearnings will exceed your earnings.

If you follow your wants in your buying, the result will be chaos. If you design your spending, then your dollars can take care of you. With a system you will probably be more satisfied, have more of what you really want, and have less financial problems. Without a strategy money matters will probably cause tension and crisis in your family.

A careful pilot of an airplane checks his supply of gas before every trip. He plots his journey with care, to make certain there will be gas enough to take him to his destination. He usually makes certain that enough gas is held in reserve to allow him time to fly to another airport in case he has bad weather and can't land where he planned. Federal Aviation Agency regulations require such planning on all instrument flights. Good sense requires such foresight on every flight. You, as a spender, will also reach more financial destinations through careful, disciplined, and planned spending—budgeting.

When each of our two daughters started to kindergarten, she began her first budget. The mechanical system consisted of three small boxes, of the same size, stapled together. Each box was labeled by category and marked by amount—SAVE, SPEND, and CHURCH.

Every week I parceled out the allowance—three nickels. One went into each box. The budget was evident; the plan was simple. Visual control was established. Even a six-year-old began to understand her planned spending.

The three-box method was adequate through high school. The amounts changed as the girls grew and as inflation roared, but the boxes continued in use as a control system. Intriguingly, the girls were seldom out of money. When they were, they knew it. No money in the box meant none to spend!

Here's a real lesson for those who continually plunge into debt by spending more than they have. A budget is the best way I know of to avoid the pitfall of too much month left over at the end of your money.

There is more to budgeting than simply planning your spending. Checkups are essential to compare the money you spend with your budget. Whether you use small boxes to maintain visual control, or a budget book to record spending, you need a record-keeping system. The principle of record keeping is well established in the Bible by this verse: "Any enterprise is built by wise planning, becomes strong through common sense, and profits wonderfully by keeping abreast of the facts" (Proverbs 24:3, 4).

Any Enterprise   That marriage is an enterprise may be a surprise. It is easy for you to add up the income from your previous years of employment. You can project your expected earnings for the years between now and retirement. Consider inflation in your figures, allowing at least the average annual inflation rate of 3.1% this country experienced in the 24 years between 1951 and 1974. That your earning and spending form a financial enterprise is a fact which your figures will clearly demonstrate.

Wise Planning   Salesmen are counseled to "plan the work and work the plan." This is good counsel for those seeking to follow God's principle of record keeping. How are your records? Where has your planning taken you?

Completion of the Financial Summary form will help you determine the present state of your financial affairs. When you have figured your Net Worth you may consider how many years have been

Financial Summary

Where We Are Now   Date_____

A. What We Own
1. Money in the bank   _____
2. Cash value of life insurance (call agent on each policy)   _____
3. Savings (Savings & Loan, Credit Union, etc.)   _____
4. Stocks and Bonds (present market value)   _____
5. Real estate
   (a) Home (current market value, less costs)   _____
   (b) Other real estate   _____
6. Other investments   _____
7. Personal possessions (for each room you have that is nicely furnished, multiply by $500)   _____
8. Automobiles (call dealer, ask for average retail value)   _____
9. Other property (boats, trailers, cabins, etc.)   _____
10. Special property (cameras, guns, hobbies, motorcycles, silver, camping equipment, stereo equipment)   _____
11. Interest in retirement or pension plan   _____

     What We Own Totals (1–4)   Cash and other savings   _____
                   (5)   Real estate   _____
                 (6–11)   Other property   _____

     Total Assets   =======

B. What We Owe	Amount Due	Monthly Payment	Estimated Annual Interest
1. To the mortgagee of our home	_____	_____	_____
2. To others			
(a) Bank	_____	_____	_____
(b) Loan company	_____	_____	_____
(c) Credit Union	_____	_____	_____
(d) Insurance companies	_____	_____	_____
3. Credit Card companies	_____	_____	_____
4. Other businesses	_____	_____	_____
5. Other (family loans, etc.)	_____	_____	_____
6. Medical, Dental, Hospital	_____	_____	_____

Total Liabilities   =======

     A. What We Own, Total Assets   _____
     B. Less What We Owe, Total Liabilities   _____
     C. Net Worth   =======
     D. Number of years of accumulation   _____
     E. Average annual accumulation of resources   =======

required to accumulate your resources. You can determine how much you have added each year to your financial Net Worth.

Common Sense "Can two walk together, except they be agreed?" (Amos 3:3 KJV). Agreement in the spending plan for the family is essential for the husband and wife. Seldom do I see a family with financial problems where there is not real tension within the marriage.

Common sense dictates common goals, which demand common effort and produce uncommon results. God's multiplication system for working together equals abundant results: "Two can accomplish more than twice as much as one, for the results can be much better" (Ecclesiastes 4:9). "Work happily together" is the first requisite for the family spending plan. (*See* Romans 12:16.)

Keeping Abreast A friend of mine says that you keep a budget so you won't fake yourself out. How can you plug the leaks in the budget if you don't know where the leaks are? Would you be satisfied if you were in the hospital with heart trouble and no one bothered to check up on your blood pressure, pulse count, and temperature?

I have seldom seen people who were successful stewards of their money who did not keep good records. And I rarely see a couple in financial trouble who are operating on a spending plan with adequate records.

Several years ago our company contracted with the telephone company for ten hours of long-distance time each month. For that minimum we paid a flat rate, plus a charge for each additional minute of use over the ten hours. All employees were aware of the objective of avoiding usage in excess of the ten hours. I started them all out with this admonition, "Do the best you can." Here are the results, in round figures, of the first three months: thirteen hours of use for the first month; sixteen hours for the second month; and nineteen hours were used the third month. By the end of the third month we were using almost twice the time we budgeted. My plan had failed; it was time for a better system.

We then instituted individual responsibility. Each employee had an allotted number of minutes he could use during the month. He was to keep track of his accumulative usage for the month. A chart was devised to show our total daily usage with everyone advised as to where we were, compared to where we planned to be. Keeping abreast of these facts, and using discipline to stay within individual quotas, our usage dropped back to ten hours the fourth month and hasn't been in excess of twelve hours yet. Record keeping allowed us to meet our objective.

One day my teenage daughter Jenny asked me, "Dad, why are we so poor? It seems I can never buy the clothes I want, and neither can Mom." My response was a lengthy lecture on how we chose to spend our income. Finally, I explained how our family operated on a clothing budget, and that there was simply not enough money there to buy at *all* times *all* the clothes *all* of us wanted.

Jenny pressed further, "How come I can't have my own budget?" Marjean and I discussed this idea privately and decided to open checking accounts for each of the teenage girls. Monthly we would deposit the budgeted amount in their accounts. They were to pay for all their own clothes as they bought them. Checks were not to be written on these accounts except for their clothes.

Prior to the personal budgeting, we had horrendous arguments whenever we said no to clothing purchases. With the responsibility shifted to each daughter and with a predetermined plan, arguments stopped.

After a few tough lessons learned from purchasing items that were too expensive and running out of money for real needs, both girls became excellent shoppers. What better way to "train up a child in the way he should go" financially, than to provide an opportunity for individual responsibility in decisions on teenage clothes?

The goal of such training for children is to steadily increase the

BLONDIE®   By Chic Young

© King Features Syndicate 1972.

financial responsibility they have. By learning individual responsibility for money, the young person is being well prepared to leave the nest.

Before you as parents can teach God's principles for money to your children, you must have attended classes yourselves. Whether you are struggling with debt or have some financial success, *you can profit* and God can reap from your keeping a budget.

8 Budgeting—The Nitty-Gritty

Convinced that a budget will benefit your family, you must now build a spending plan for your needs. Estimating expenditures for a year at a time is the place to start. Here's a three-step process to help you:

Step A Review the categories on the list, Our Financial Goals. The purpose of estimating your expenditures is to arrive at an annual and

Our Financial Goals

	Monthly	Annually
1. Tithes and Offerings	————	————
2. Federal Income Tax	————	————
3. State Income Tax	————	————
4. Social Security Tax	————	————
5. Other Taxes (such as City)	————	————
6. Shelter	————	————
7. Food	————	————
8. Clothing	————	————
9. Health	————	————
10. Education	————	————
11. Life Insurance	————	————
12. Gifts	————	————
13. Transportation	————	————
14. Personal Allowances	————	————
15. Vacations	————	————
16. Savings	————	————
17. Household Purchases	————	————
18. Debt Reduction	————	————
19.	————	————
20.	————	————
Total	═══	═══

monthly figure for each spending category. Are there other categories you need in your budget? Are there categories you do not need? Make any necessary changes on this form, so that it meets your family's requirements.

Step B   Fill in the monthly or annual column of each category you are using on Our Financial Goals. The explanations which follow will guide you in arriving at amounts for each spending category. Start with the first item and work through them in order. Remember that a journey of a thousand miles begins with the first step. If you have a monthly estimate, multiply it by twelve for the annual figures. If you have an annual figure, divide it by twelve for the monthly figure. You may need to refer to your checkbook to obtain previous expenditures so you can make accurate estimates of future amounts.

1. Tithes and Offerings—all charitable giving: church, United Way, etc.
2. Federal Income Tax—all amounts withheld, plus estimates paid, plus any amounts due with tax return.
3. State Income Tax—all amounts withheld, plus estimates paid, plus any amounts due with tax return.
4. Social Security Tax—5.85% of your first $15,300 earned; total for year $895.05; same for your spouse; 7.90% if you are self-employed. These are 1976 figures.
5. Other Taxes—taxes on your wages, such as city income taxes.
6. Shelter
   (a) If renting include rent, heat, lights, telephone, household supplies, appliance repairs, other home-related expenses.
   (b) If buying include house payments, interest, insurance, real-estate taxes, repairs and maintenance, other items listed under renting.
7. Food—grocery-store items, paper goods, cleaning supplies, pet foods. Include all eating-out and carry-out items and school lunches. It may also include entertainment.
8. Clothing—purchases, cleaning, repairs. This may be divided with a separate budget for each family member.
9. Health—health insurance premiums, medical, dental, hospital expenses, drug items, medicines, cosmetics.

10. Education—school expenses, books, lessons, college expenses, uniforms, equipment, subscriptions to newspapers and magazines.

11. Life Insurance—all premiums, whether paid monthly, quarterly, or annually.

12. Gifts—birthdays, anniversaries, special occasions, Christmas, weddings, funerals, office collections, dues for organizations.

13. Transportation—gas, oil, repairs, licenses, personal property tax, insurance. Car payments or an amount set aside to purchase your next car.

14. Personal Allowances—for each family member to spend personally. Hair care, recreation, baby-sitting, hobbies, and children's allowances.

15. Vacations—trips, camps, weekend outings; trips for weddings, funerals, and family visits.

16. Savings—amounts set aside now for future needs.

17. Household Purchases—for major appliances, furniture, carpeting, and major home maintenance such as roofing and painting.

18. Debt Reduction—includes all payments on debt not included in other categories such as: school loans, amounts due relatives, banks, or others.

19. Special Categories—anything tailored to your own needs or desires; this may include a boat, cabin, airplane, or hobby.

Step C After filling in all of the monthly and annual estimates, add the totals. *Wow!* The totals are greater than your income! Right? Right!! If so, you are not unusual. Every budget I've ever seen starts out with wants in excess of income.

Now! The fun and prayers start. What are your needs? What are your wants? Here are some hints and guidelines to help you.

Shelter—not over 30% of your gross income. If gross income is $1,000 monthly, all expenses for shelter should not exceed $300. If you are over in this area, you may need to secure a cheaper living situation in order to balance your budget.

Food—as high as 30% with less than a $700 monthly income to less than 20% for $1,500 income.

Clothing—not over 10% of your income.

Short-term debt—not to exceed 10% of your monthly take-home pay times 18. With a monthly net income of $750 the debt limit would be $75 × 18 = $1,350. This figure would not include a mortgage on your home. The experts all say that you are headed for trouble if your short-term monthly debt payments exceed 20% of your take-home pay. Thus, with a take-home pay of $750, you are in real financial trouble if your monthly payments for debt exceed $150, excluding a home mortgage.

All successful budgets have one thing in common: the outgo is *not* greater than the income! God's guidance is essential as you begin together the painful surgical process of cutting back your spending plans to match your income. Have you prayed? You need God's wisdom. Ask Him for it.

Now, examine each spending category. Ask these questions: Which expenses are essential? Which can you do without? Which can you reduce?

During the energy crisis we learned that we could reduce heat, light, driving, and recreation without serious effects on the quality of our living. Since most of us eat too much for our own good, a reduction in food consumption can actually lead to improved health. Steak or hamburgers cooked by the husband on the barbecue at home occasionally, and served by candlelight, can be just as enjoyable as a meal out—and far more economical.

Family togetherness can be enhanced by spending an evening making gifts in assembly-line fashion for Christmas and other occasions. Just before Christmas a college student from our church told me that she had made her own presents. She said that on a college student's budget she couldn't afford to buy them. Her estimate was that ten gifts could be made for the money it took to buy one.

Spending for Christmas and special occasions very often blows the family budget. In a family of four, one gift for each occasion—Christmas, birthdays, anniversaries, Valentine's Day, and Easter—can easily add up to eighteen to twenty-four gifts. When you add the relatives and friends, you can be involved in purchasing up to fifty presents a year. Using family talents in creative projects can result in substantial financial savings while you are giving to others a one-of-a-kind expression of your love.

Major changes may be necessary in your family patterns. One friend had accumulated four weeks of vacation each year. He had also accumulated substantial debt. Part of the overspending was caused by his family's concept that a vacation meant trips out of town—with the resultant costs of driving, eating out, motels, recreation, and purchases of curios. That family needed to plan creative vacations where additional family income could be earned, home maintenance could be accomplished, and creative money-saving projects completed. Visualize the difference in long-term family welfare between those two contrasting types of vacations.

Yes, the surgical process of trimming the family budget is painful. So is the Christian walk! Jesus instructed us clearly about the way we choose in every area of our lives: "Enter by the narrow gate; for the gate is wide and the way is easy, that leads to destruction, and those who enter by it are many. For the gate is narrow and the way is hard, that leads to life, and those who find it are few" (Matthew 7:13, 14 RSV).

The wide financial path is easy; no money down and an easy-payment plan. Buy what you want when you want it. CHARGE IT! Don't bother with budgets and record keeping. Such thinking maps out the road to destruction.

God's financial way is hard. Self-denial, discipline, and sacrifice are the marks of a Christian and his money. God's stewardship calls for wise and knowledgeable use of our money. This means a plan and records to help you stay within the plan. God's abundance is not found in overspending what He provides for us, but in His blessing us as we are faithful with what He gives us.

Keep praying and cutting until your expenses are within your income. Remember, if your spending plan won't work on paper, it won't work—period.

To set up your budget, you need only a simple booklet. Most bookstores carry inexpensive account books for family-budget purposes. The budget page shown on the following page is typical; as an illustration let's consider the category of Shelter.

Budget Illustration

Shelter (*left page*)   (*right page*) Shelter

¼	Deposit	360	00	360	00	¼	Deposit	360	00	360	00
²⁄₁	Deposit	360	00	720	00	¼	Envelope	15	00	345	00
						⅓	ABC Mortgage Co.	210	40	134	60
						⅓	Soft Water Co.	6	95	127	65
						⅛	Local Electric Co.	20	32	107	33
						¹⁄₁₀	Wet Water Co.	13	21	94	12
						¹⁄₁₄	Slick TV Repair Co.	24	32	69	80
						¹⁄₂₀	Appliance Repair Co.	26	00	43	80
						¹⁄₂₈	Bell Telephone Co.	23	80	20	00
						²⁄₁	Deposit	360	00	380	00

Since the procedure for recording expenditures in each spending category is similar, a thorough explanation of one category will suffice for you to learn how to budget. Your money will be spent in two ways—cash and checks. Your record system will keep track of each check by category and show cash balances in each category. Each category has two pages. The left page shows your plan, and each month the total spending goal for that category is entered. Refer to the Budget Illustration and follow each item as it is explained.

1. On the left page enter the date of the first of the month in which you start your budget. Show the source of your entry—Deposit. Show the amount you plan to spend for Shelter and show the amount of your planned spending in Shelter for the year to date. In our first entry the plan is to allow $360 monthly for Shelter; the date is entered. The source of the entry is Deposit, and a cumulative total each month will show the amount spent for the year to date.

The right page shows your plan and records your spending. Thus, you can see how your spending compares with your plan at any given time. This is *reality*.

2. On the right page, duplicate entry 1. This entry establishes your intention to spend $360 for Shelter during January (or whichever month you choose to start). You could maintain this budget by having a separate checking account for each spending category, but this would be expensive and impractical. Visualize, as you post to this Shelter account, that you are accomplishing the same thing as if you had separate bank accounts. The postings are expenditures from the account, and the declining balance after each purchase is similar to the declining balance in your checkbook as you write checks.

3. You are now ready to post the cash envelope deposit of $15. Cash control is accomplished by setting aside some cash each month to cover the small purchases. These would be items not normally paid for by check. In Shelter, such items might include: home-repair items such as bolts, glass, or putty; garden needs such as seed or bug spray; and household-maintenance products such as light bulbs, paint, or wax. A stationery envelope may be used to hold the cash. On the front of the envelope write the spending category, such as Shelter in this example.

A check for cash in the amount of your estimate would be written. Estimate that $15 would be used for cash expenditures; the money is placed in the Shelter envelope. As cash is spent by family members they come to the envelope to get reimbursed for the expenditure. No individual expenditures are recorded for this cash since we are not interested in where each dollar goes. It is sufficient to know that $15 was allotted to cash items in Shelter during the month. If you actually spend only $10 cash from the envelope during a month, the next month you could allocate only $10 to this envelope, bringing it back to your original $15 cash position.

The key to the cash-envelope system is to have sufficient cash with you to make these small purchases. The way to be prepared is to carry a set amount of cash with you at all times. My wife and I have each carried $20 with us as working capital. As I spend small amounts of this $20 I write it down in my pocket notebook, indicating the date, purpose, and amount. Periodically I get these amounts back from the envelopes at home so that my $20 is intact again. If I start with a set amount of cash, I know how much I am short when I neglect to write down an amount spent. For example, if I bought nails for the house that cost $2.48, I'd make a note like this in my personal notebook: 1/3—Nails—$2.48. Upon returning home I would get the $2.48 from the Shelter envelope, and once again have my $20 intact. No record is kept of the money removed from each envelope. But our guide in this has been Luke 16:10 (RSV), "He who is faithful in a very little is faithful also in much; and he who is dishonest in a very little is dishonest also in much." You can cheat yourselves by shuffling cash between the envelopes.

Since you have written a check for the $15 (and probably cash sufficient for all the other envelopes in a single check), you post to the Shelter account the amount you put into the Shelter envelope. (It is a good idea to get dollar bills for the envelopes in order to have change available to replace your working capital.) Now the $15 is subtracted from the $360 to show the amount of $345 still available this month in the Shelter account.

4. From your check stub, record the date and amount of the mortgage payment on your home. Subtract the amount of this payment ($210.40) from the balance in this account, showing an amount of $134.60 still available for Shelter. Additional postings are made from your check stubs in the same manner to include soft water, electricity, water, television repair, telephone service, gas or fuel costs for heating, and others that will pertain to your household.

The last entry begins the new month as you start the process all over again. Note that you ended the month with $20 of your plan not spent. *Rejoice!* You'll probably need it later. A careful examination of your month may sometimes reveal that no payment was made to one of the utility companies. A computer may have stalled, and you failed to receive a bill. Don't worry, you won't get it free! Just expect a double bill the next month.

Most of your accounts will have certain amounts that will be paid in large chunks during a single month. The Gift category is an example where you could build a surplus all year until you purchase Christmas gifts. Shelter costs may include an annual insurance premium, so you will need to build up a surplus in order to meet that premium. Certain accounts may show that they are overspent for a few months. If an annual life-insurance premium comes due in March in the amount of $360, you may have allocated only $90 in your Insurance category by the time you pay the premium. Thus, the balance in life insurance would be overdrawn by $270 at the end of March. As long as you are not *over*spending, a negative balance need not disturb you, as in the case of the life-insurance example. But a negative balance in your food, clothing, gifts, transportation, allowances, vacations, or household purchases should be a loud danger signal. A deficit balance should only be tolerated if it can be explained on the basis of an annual planned expenditure. Any other reason should be grounds for emergency cutting in that category until you are able to balance the account again.

The Food account has been handled in a slightly different way in our family. Marjean carries a separate coin purse with her. When she buys groceries at the store and cashes a check for more than the amount of the purchase, she places the unspent change in that purse. She uses that change for her next grocery purchases, children's lunches and eating-out. When the cash is gone, she cashes another check and follows the same procedure. The basic difference is that she carries the food money with her wherever she goes.

A potential snag in food costs is the husband's lunches. We have allocated an amount for my lunches out of our food budget. This amount is placed in an envelope so that I, too, am forced to economize on my lunches. Most men are overweight and fight the battle of the bulge. It is a real act of love for the husband to eat a light lunch at noon so he can freely enjoy his wife's lovingly prepared evening meal. Such sacrificial lunches can also have a significant impact on the monthly spending for food.

A budget will force real communication. Complete honesty is required. The two most frequent sources of trouble that I've found are the hairdresser for the wife and the man's recreation, whether it's golf, hunting, or photography. Often, when I am involved in financial counseling with couples regarding money trouble, I learn that the wife makes a regular, weekly trip to the hairdresser for the works! The furniture may be threadbare, but still she goes. Emotions can really get charged on this one. Or, the husband may be a tightwad in home management, clothes for the kids, and gifts, but he never hesitates to go off with the guys on some expensive trip and purchase whatever new gadget and outfit fits the occasion.

My recommendation for a solution to these and other potentially explosive areas is having a personal allowance. As you develop your spending plan, keep these individual items in mind. We decided early in our marriage that our personal allowance was to be spent as we each pleased. We were not to be accountable to each other for it. If Marjean wanted to go to the beauty shop, she could do so as long as the allowance held out. I could play golf as often as I liked, if I had the allowance to pay for it. We each paid our own way for entertainment—a practice we still follow.

WARNING: BE PREPARED FOR TEARS. We still remember one New Year's Eve when we stayed home. I chose that night as a time to post our budget book and see how we finished the year. With little tact I pointed out to Marjean how much *she* had overspent for food. Tears flowed—the evening was ruined.

In twenty-one years of budgeting we've had our frustrations and tears, but our budget has saved us thousands of dollars. And we have that savings now, at the time our daughters need it for college.

More importantly, we've communicated together in an area that is a leading cause of divorce. As we've learned to work together on the choices involved in spending our money, we've built a successful base for our marriage. Harmony in our money has encouraged us to work for unity in all other areas of our lives together. You, too, can profit by maintaining a family spending plan.

BLONDIE   By Chic Young

9 Nest Eggs

When a natural or artificial egg is left in a nest to induce a hen or other bird to lay or continue laying eggs there, it is called a *nest egg*. The implication is that this egg, by virtue of its placement, will result in further production.

Someone has said that everyone should have two aims in life: to make a little money first, and to make a little money last. Money that is set aside to last until it is needed at a future date is usually called a *nest egg*.

That a nest egg is meant to be productive is illustrated by the Parable of the Talents as told by our Lord in Matthew 25:14–30. The first two men were given the most money and used that money to double their master's investment. It is interesting to note that in their cases the investments did not double without effort on their part. In verses 16 and 17 of the Living Bible we see that: "The man who received the $5,000 began immediately to buy and sell with it and soon earned another $5,000. The man with $2,000 went right to work, too, and earned another $2,000." The third man, however, hid the money he received in a hole in the ground for safekeeping. In the story he is condemned for not investing the money so that it could at least have earned some interest. His reproof is in verses 26 and 27: "But his master replied, 'Wicked man! Lazy slave! Since you knew I would demand your profit, you should at least have put my money into the bank so I could have some interest.'"

Interest is not paid on money, but on what money does. Thus we see clearly the distinction between savings and investments. Savings are funds set aside out of income; they are monies that are not spent. If the savings are hidden under the mattress, they continue to be savings. When those savings are entrusted to others, or put to work to produce a profit or income or both, then they become an *investment*.

My own definition of an *investment* is the turning-over of some property or resource to another person or form, expecting a profit or an increase. We see this expectation from an investment in the Parable of the Talents. The man turned over some of his money to the three men, expecting to get his money back (safety of principal) and an increase in his investment (appreciation and or interest).

Prerequisites to Financial Investments:

Give at least a tithe to the Lord.   "You must tithe all of your crops every year" (Deuteronomy 14:22). Don't expect God to bless your financial investments if you are robbing Him of the tithes which are rightfully His.

Pay off your debts.   If you are investing money that rightfully is due others, then you really are investing money for others without their permission. The principle in the Scripture is to pay your debts first, before investing your money: "Don't withhold repayment of your debts. Don't say 'some other time,' if you can pay now" (Proverbs 3:27, 28).

Commit your financial investments to God.   Give up all your rights to your assets. Dedicate your investments to His glory, to be used for His purposes. He is trustworthy. While suffering in jail, Paul expressed his complete trust in Christ in this way: ". . . for I know the one in whom I trust, and I am sure that he is able to safely guard all that I have given him until the day of his return" (2 Timothy 1:12). And He is the best investment manager of all.

Why Invest Money?

To plan ahead.   "A sensible man watches for problems ahead and prepares to meet them. The simpleton never looks, and suffers the consequences" (Proverbs 27:12).

I am appalled at the number of Christians who violate this principle. I know several who have seen that their youngsters were in a church that preached the gospel. They have tried to provide a fine home (in most cases, even cars during high school) for their children. However, when the time came for the youngster to attend college, no money had been set aside to pay for an education in a private Christian school or even to provide funds to leave home and attend a public institution. In every case I know of, it was not because of a lack of income on the part of the parents. The irony is that if the income of the parents had been low enough, the youngster would have been able to secure a scholarship or a tuition grant to help with college expenses. The parents had placed more emphasis on "things" during the formative years than on laying aside money to provide for college expenses when that time arrived.

To provide for your family in time of need. "But anyone who won't care for his own relatives when they need help, especially those living in his own family, has no right to say he is a Christian. Such a person is worse than the heathen" (1 Timothy 5:8).

A boy in our tenth-grade Sunday-school class has learned much already about providing for his own family. His father, through sharing the Word of God with him, taught him about tithing. While working as a busboy in a local cafe during high school, this boy earned $150 monthly. Every month he knew the joy of giving. He sent $5.00 to his church, $5.00 to his needy grandfather in Florida, and $5.00 to the Billy Graham Evangelistic Association. (He had told me that the Billy Graham television programs had a real ministry in his life.) This young man was already following God's commandments to care for his own family.

Statistics reveal that most men do not save money. As a result, they reach the sunset years of life with little or no income. Look at Table 7 on the next page to discover the fortune that will be earned between the first and last paychecks.

Since so many earn fortunes, you would think that men in their preretirement years would accumulate substantial assets. The facts prove otherwise. A Social Security Administration study revealed that 50% of married men aged 58–63 had financial assets of less

Table 7: Total Earnings to Age 65

	Average Monthly Income		
Age	$500	$1,000	$1,500
25	$240,000	$480,000	$720,000
30	210,000	420,000	630,000
35	180,000	360,000	540,000
40	150,000	300,000	450,000
45	120,000	240,000	360,000
50	90,000	180,000	270,000
55	60,000	120,000	180,000

than $2,116. (This figure excludes property equity.) The conclusion drawn is: "Even for the relatively 'well-off' married men, however, such a nest egg is obviously not large enough to produce any sizeable income or be converted into cash that could sustain an adequate standard of living for very long" (*Social Security Bulletin,* August 1973). "Relatively 'well-off' married men" is stated because the same survey revealed that 50% of nonmarried men aged 58–63 had financial assets of less than $470.

Providing for your family in time of need means saving now. A prudent plan for managing your income, so that a regular nest egg is built, should provide money for unforeseen emergencies, retirement living, and an inheritance for your children.

The enemy of the nest egg is procrastination. Note the excuses of those who always seem to put off saving money till later.

AGES 25–30: I can't save now. I'm just getting started and my income is low.

AGES 30–40: I can't save now. I have a young family to raise.

AGES 40–50: I can't save now. I have two children in college.

AGES 50–60: I can't save now. My wife and I want to enjoy life.

AGES 60–65: I can't save enough between now and retirement time to make much difference.

AGES 65 AND OVER: I can't save now. I'm living with my son and his wife.

Mishandling our personal finances is grounds for disqualification for a church responsibility. Paul writes: "He must manage his own household well, keeping his children submissive and respectful in every way; for if a man does not know how to manage his own household, how can he care for God's church?" (1 Timothy 3:4, 5 RSV). The idea here is very clear. Mismanaging family finances disqualifies us for holding leadership positions in the church. No wonder many churches are in spiritual and financial trouble.

Investing our savings proves our faithfulness and provides for future contingencies, family emergencies, and inheritances for our children. God is pleased when we honor Him by saving and investing.

Investments Are Not Without Dangers.

You may begin to trust in financial resources instead of trusting God. Proverbs clearly warns: "Trust in your money and down you go! Trust in God and flourish as a tree!" (Proverbs 11:28). "The rich man thinks of his wealth as an impregnable defense, a high wall of safety. What a dreamer!" (Proverbs 18:11).

You may become entangled with your investments. Some of the investor's time and energy is usually required for the monitoring of financial resources. Paul's warning in Timothy is clear: "And as Christ's soldier do not let yourself become tied up in wordly affairs, for then you cannot satisfy the one who has enlisted you in his army" (2 Timothy 2:4). Woe that I should not be able to satisfy Christ with my life because of a consuming interest in financial investments! "Don't weary yourself trying to get rich. Why waste your time? For riches can disappear as though they had the wings of a bird!" (Proverbs 23:4, 5).

Your investments may lead you to increased temptations. Rapidly increasing assets may tempt you to personal pride. Or you may react to a sudden or extensive decrease in your assets with moodiness or depression. Paul covers these conditions precisely: "For men who set their hearts on being wealthy expose themselves to temptation. They fall into a trap and lay themselves open to all sorts of silly and wicked desires, which are quite capable of utterly ruining and destroying their souls. For loving money leads to all kinds of evil, and some men in the struggle to be rich have lost their faith and caused themselves agonies of mind" (1 Timothy 6:9, 10 PHILLIPS).

You may develop a desire to get money.   Such desire usually renders a Christian useless. Jesus is concerned about the heart-attitude of a man. No matter how much a man has, if he has an overwhelming desire to get rich, then he is serving the god of money instead of our God. Jesus sums this up: "But all too quickly the attractions of this world and the delights of wealth, and the search for success and lure of nice things come in and crowd out God's message from their hearts, so that no crop is produced" (Mark 4:19).

Just as no financial investment is without some risk, the very process of saving money also carries a degree of spiritual risk. Scriptural warnings help us develop right attitudes toward investing.

How Shall We Invest the Nest Eggs?

An understanding of the prerequisites of investment and a commitment to God's pattern for investing brings us to the question of how and where shall we invest the nest eggs?

The old investment adage is: DON'T PUT ALL YOUR EGGS IN ONE BASKET. The city of Wichita, Kansas, would have done well to have followed that admonition when trees were planted along its streets. Someone decided the ideal tree for Wichita was the Dutch elm. Thousands of Dutch elms were planted throughout the city. As they grew they lined the streets and provided shade in our neighborhoods, making our city among the most shaded in the nation. Suddenly, like a thief in the night the Dutch-elm disease came. There was no known preventive and no known cure. Now, up and down the streets there are many gaps where the trees have already died and been removed. Other trees look sick; a few are still strong and sturdy, but their days are numbered. No matter what the eggs are, putting them all into one basket is a most hazardous way.

My idea of investments is to diversify according to these priorities: (1) life insurance, (2) business or profession, (3) house, (4) deferred compensation, and (5) other investments.

Life insurance is first because that's the only way I know for most of us to provide for our families in the event of our own death. Whether you buy term insurance or whole-life insurance should depend upon your own analysis of the costs and benefits of each kind.

The *Readers' Guide to Periodical Literature* in your local library could lead you to excellent articles on the subject (such as "Term Insurance *vs.* Whole Life," (*Forbes,* March 15, 1975). What is right for one person may be wrong for another.

Your business or profession should rank next as an investment. Your own education is an investment of time and money that should pay excellent returns during your working years.

If you decide to be in business for yourself, your own efforts will largely determine the success or failure of the business. The Small Business Administration states that there are approximately 9.2 million small businesses operating, so you have plenty of successful examples to encourage you. You must also recognize the great risk in starting your own company. Dun & Bradstreet, Inc. states, ". . . in recent years, more than 400,000 firms have been started annually . . . between 350,000 and 400,000 discontinued . . . ." Of the thousands of businesses that fail, Dun & Bradstreet, Inc. says, "The first five years are the hardest—57% of all concerns going under in 1973 were in operation five years or less."

A principle in Scripture is to invest in your business, which will be productive, then build your house: "Develop your business first before building your house" (Proverbs 24:27). Most people reverse this. The large house, purchased early in life, tends to involve so much of their money that investing in a business is out of the question.

If you work for a company, you may be involved in its pension or profit-sharing plan. Funds are set aside for you now, without deductions for social security or income taxes. If you are self-employed or work for a company that has no retirement plan, you may qualify for your own individual retirement account. It is possible to set up a savings account on which you pay no tax on the income saved now or on the annual interest earned by your savings. Taxable withdrawals are planned for retirement age in such a way that the potential tax savings may be significant. Consult a financial specialist for details.

Other areas of investments are almost as varied as the imagination can stretch. Real estate, oil, commodities, stocks, bonds, antiques, stamps, coins, jewelry, art, rare books, artifacts, guns, bottles, dolls, or virtually anything people collect can be considered investments. Some of these, such as stocks, bonds, and real estate, pay a return on an annual basis. Others are held with the expectation that they will increase in value as time goes by.

Your investments beyond life insurance, business, and home should be teamed with your own interests and personality. If you were raised on a farm and have a knowledge of agricultural products, the intricacies of weather, price variables of feed and fertilizer, and you enjoy keeping abreast of the farm situation, then you might pursue a lifelong interest in agricultural investments. These could include everything from commodity purchases to owning and acquiring farmland. If common stocks are your interest, you might specialize in a study of those companies that are primarily agriculturally oriented. Or you might own a herd of cattle or hogs.

I chose to pursue the area of common stocks. By reading annual reports of companies I have invested in, I am able to keep abreast of a cross-section of American business. Most annual reports share not only the past history, but also the goals and objectives for the future. As a businessman, these are interesting to me; they also give me vision and ideas for my own small business.

Another friend of mine enjoyed working on old houses as a means of relaxation. He bought houses close to where he lived and fixed them up for renting. They provided work opportunities for his boys as they grew up. When the youngsters left home, the houses had appreciated in value. Since my friend's interests had now changed, he sold the properties at a substantial gain.

All these investments that we have discussed are the kind that lend themselves to systematic investing. The regular monthly payment on the home for a twenty-year mortgage results in having a home completely paid for. Yearly whole-life insurance premiums not only provide insurance in case of sudden death, but also add up to retirement values. Steady hard work in your own business often results in a substantial salable asset. The key to investing in the stock market is to set aside regular amounts for systematic investment.

I have never been successful in knowing when the market was too high or too low. In fact, figures prove that most individual investors buy high and sell low. After all, it takes real courage to buy when the stock market is low, the news is bad, and the future looks bleak. That's the time when most individuals sell out. But the Bible says:

"Steady plodding brings prosperity; hasty speculation brings poverty" (Proverbs 21:5). Setting aside money regularly to invest in the stock market means that when the market is down you will buy more shares with your money. When the market is up, you will buy fewer shares. By investing steadily, you are doing what is called *dollar cost averaging*. If you believe in the long-term financial future of America and the world, this is one way to express that belief.

An illustration of dollar cost averaging will reveal its principle and its power. Assume the price of a stock selling at $10 a share drops 50%—obviously a bad situation. Even worse, assume you had bought $100 worth at $10 per share—obviously bad timing. But also assume you invested $100 at each point of change thereafter as the stock dropped all the way to $5 and then recovered to $10. This is not a roaring bull-market example—yet, what happened overall was very satisfactory.

$100 Invested Each Point Down the Ladder and Each Point Back Up

Bought 10.000 shs. at $10	$10 = 10.000 shs.
11.111 shs. at $9	$9 = 11.111 shs.
12.500 shs. at $8	$8 = 12.500 shs.
14.286 shs. at $7	$7 = 14.286 shs.
16.667 shs. at $6	$6 = 16.667 shs.
	$5 = 20.000 shs.

Total Invested	$1,100.00
Total shares bought = 149.128	
End value (149.128 × $10)	$1,491.28
Total Gain = 35.6%	

Remember, at no point did the stock ever sell above your initial price—but in the end you had a 35% profit. And this does not include whatever dividends the stock might have paid. This is the value of dollar cost averaging!

The above table is, of course, hypothetical. An investor should realize that no investment program can assure a profit or protect against loss in declining markets. He would incur a loss if he discontinues the program during a period when the market value of his shares is less than his cost. For this reason, any investor contemplating such a program should take into account his ability to continue it during any such period. However, the figures do provide comfort to those who assume that what comes down will go back up.

Is it not also reasonable to assume that what goes up may come back down? I wanted to see what the same illustration would reveal for the dollar-averager who started buying his shares when they were low, continued buying up to $10, and bought all the way back down to where he started. Here's the comparison:

$100 Invested Each Point Up the Ladder and Each Point Back Down

Bought 20.000 shs. at $5	$5 = 20.000 shs.
16.667 shs. at $6	$6 = 16.667 shs.
14.286 shs. at $7	$7 = 14.286 shs.
12.500 shs. at $8	$8 = 12.500 shs.
11.111 shs. at $9	$9 = 11.111 shs.
$10 = 10.000 shs.	

Total Invested	$1,100.00
Total shares bought = 149.128	
End value (149.128 × $5)	$745.64
Total Loss = 32.2%	

Timing in any investment is crucial. If you invested steadily, as in the above illustration, and had to sell when the stock was back down to $5, you would have lost 32.2% of your investment. I have not found any way to avoid risk in investments. Don't get me wrong, I'm not knocking the steady-plodding principle in investments. But no method that I know of *guarantees* a riskless investment. At the time you want or need to sell any holding, it may be worth more or less than you paid for it. The value will be determined entirely by what the buyer wants to pay you for your holding.

Of course, as a Christian, I realize that everything we see will burn someday. "The day of the Lord is surely coming, as unexpectedly as a thief, and then the heavens will pass away with a terrible noise and the heavenly bodies will disappear in fire, and the earth and everything on it will be burned up" (2 Peter 3:10). But for now, I do live in this world, and I am called to be faithful in what God has given me.

We are warned in Scripture to avoid get-rich-quick investments. "The man who speculates is soon back to where he began—with nothing. This, as I said, is a very serious problem, for all his hard work has been for nothing; he has been working for the wind. It is all swept away. All the rest of his life he is under a cloud—gloomy, discouraged, frustrated, and angry" (Ecclesiastes 5:15–17). There is no way I could warn you more clearly against get-rich-quick schemes than the Bible has done. Yet, millions of dollars are lost each year to fraudulent deals because of the greed of investors.

The salesperson who pressures you to BUY NOW should trigger a red warning flag in your mind. Consider the "friend" who drops by to give you an opportunity to "invest" in a red-hot oil deal. Unfortunately, you must decide tonight because "they are going to start drilling in the morning."

There is an understandable reason for so many mistakes in financial matters by Christians. We know little about the complicated nature of life insurance and all of its variables, to say nothing of the hundreds of companies from which one may purchase insurance. If we go into a small business, we usually do it with no previous small-business experience, at least from an owner's point of view. Even purchasing a home is an occasional experience for most people. Except for the professional investor, those who invest in anything could certainly be considered rank amateurs.

Most people make major financial expenditures without really looking at all the facts. Such action is downright dangerous and certainly not smart. "What a shame—yes, how stupid!—to decide before knowing the facts!" (Proverbs 18:13). The ultimate cost and alternative possibilities are seldom considered when someone is being swept along in a desire to acquire a new home, car, business, or investment. It is not usually comfortable to seek counsel, as most of us want to do what we want to do when we want to do it. It is possible that the counselor might suggest that the step is not a good one for us. Then we are in the position of doing it anyway, in spite of the godly counsel we have sought. Or we have to give up our own desire, which is seldom easy.

One of the best investments that I ever made has been in a relationship. By the grace of God I developed a relationship with a Christian life-insurance counselor. He has given me counsel in life insurance as well as other areas of my life. As a competent life-insurance man, he is aware of the trends in taxation, business, wills, trusts, and profit-sharing programs. His counsel in each area has been substantial. In addition, he performs an annual review of my financial situation. Through skillful questioning concerning my future goals, he has stimulated some significant analysis in several areas of my life.

What joy it is to pray regularly with my counselor, share in Christian service with him, and know that the financial counsel he provides comes out of a mutual love for me and a common fellowship with the Lord Jesus Christ. When I say that this relationship has been an investment, I can truthfully say that it has taken effort to keep the relationship growing, but it has born fruit in both our lives.

Your most effective counselors will be those who know you best. Developing relationships with men who are competent in several areas can be an excellent investment. Godly counsel is a must for the Christian investor.

The hatching of your nest eggs should not be left to chance. For each egg to accomplish the greatest financial benefit, you must know what to expect when they hatch.

10   When the Eggs Hatch

A good egg hatches sooner or later. Your nest egg may be the source of many possibilities for your mature years. You will notice that retirement has not been mentioned.

Just as he was preparing to change from his full-time college professor status, Dr. Elton Trueblood said he was looking forward to retirement as a time to do those things for which he had prepared during his lifetime. During a speech to the annual meeting of the Wichita Chamber of Commerce, he asked this perceptive question, "Can you imagine retiring and moving to Florida to play shuffleboard the rest of your life?" Sunny leisure was not Dr. Trueblood's idea for his mature years.

Your own plans for your later years may not be formulated. A preview of the potential income from your planned nest eggs can be profitable in two ways.

1. *For financial planning.*   A realistic view of your income possibilities may surprise you. They certainly have surprised me. Your income may be insufficient for you to cease all work for pay. Or your income may support you in such a way that your financial freedom will allow tremendous opportunities for Christian service.

2. *For stimulating provocative questions about your future.*   How can the Lord best use my gifts then? What can I do now to prepare for my ministry then? What would I do if I had the expected amount of income now and didn't need to do my present work to produce it?

Do I need to make adjustments now in order to increase my expected income then? You will probably have several questions of your own.

Depending on which nest eggs you have when you reach age 65, you may have income from one or more of at least four sources: social security, life insurance, company retirement program, and personal investments.

There will be many variables in these estimates. Of course, changes each year in your circumstances will vary your figures. But you can investigate your situation in order to complete your own chart.

Social Security If you earn the maximum amount covered by social security for the next 20 years at the present benefit schedule, you may expect a monthly income on retirement at age 65 of over $427. If your wife is also 65, she will receive an additional amount equal to one-half of your benefits. Thus, your total monthly income from social security has a potential of over $640.

You may anticipate increases, as they are already built into the system. In recent years social security benefits have increased much faster than the cost of living. And under present federal tax laws, this income is not taxable by either federal or state governments.

Social security changes have been frequent in the past. Changes will continue in the future. To figure your specific situation, a visit to the nearest Social Security Administration office is recommended. To estimate your future benefits based on the current benefit scales, request a copy of the leaflet, "Estimating Your Social Security Retirement Check," from any such office.

Life Insurance The person who buys whole-life insurance has several options upon retirement. To illustrate those options, several assumptions will be made. Still, there would be differences with each company as well as other possible variables.

According to a recent survey, the average amount of personal life insurance in force for a male living in Kansas is $17,510. The gross premium for whole-life bought at age 35 would be $396 annually. Using dividends to reduce premiums over the next 30 years (assuming purchased through a mutual company), the average net premium would be $210. Such future dividends are in no way guaranteed but are projected by the company based on past experience.

At age 65 you, the policy holder, would have three main options, assuming you chose to discontinue paying premiums (which incidentally would reduce your spending). Following are the three options:

1. Hold a paid-up insurance policy in the amount of $13,080. This means that no further premiums are paid. When the insured dies, $13,080 is paid to the beneficiary.

2. Use the $9,420 cash value to purchase an annuity, which at 1974 rates will guarantee a monthly income of $73.58 for life. The annuity guarantees 120 payments to you or your beneficiary.

3. Take out the cash value of $9,420 and invest it yourself. When you cash in your policy, the difference between your cost ($6,300) and your value ($9,420) would be taxable income ($3,120). The sum remaining after taxes can either be invested to yield interest, which you can spend, or it can be set up in a monthly withdrawal plan of principal and interest for a predetermined number of years. Assume you pay the taxes, add money to bring this nest egg to $10,000, and invest it yourself. If you plan to spend only the income, you will have available $41.67 per month if your $10,000 earns 5%. If you invest $10,000 at 5% with planned withdrawals of principal, you can withdraw $106 monthly for the next ten years before running out of money. (You will have withdrawn $12,720.) After that time you will have no more funds to take out.

For our illustration, used later in the chapter, we'll assume you convert your policy to an annuity, with payments of $73.58 guaranteed for ten years, but payable for your lifetime.

Company Pension Plan There are as many varieties of company retirement programs as there are companies. Our purpose is to encourage you to look at your benefits now. What might you expect to receive in benefits when you retire?

Our assumption for this illustration is that the plan is expected to produce $6.00 per month of pension for every year of service with the company. The monthly pension at age 65 would total $120 for 20 years of service.

A normal objective is for the worker's pension plus his own social security to produce 50% to 60% of his normal earnings in retirement benefits. These pension benefits are usually taxable except to the extent of the employee's own contributions to the plan.

Personal Investments You may want to know how much money you will have in 20 years if you start now to invest a specific amount each month. A bank can provide tables showing you the growth of monthly deposits at selected rates of interest, compounded semi-annually. Table 8 shows some examples of the growth of planned savings.

Table 8: Growth of Monthly Deposits
(In Dollars)

5% Interest

Years	$1	$5	$10	$25	$50
1	12.33	61.64	123.27	308.18	616.36
5	68.20	341.00	682.01	1,705.01	3,410.03
10	155.50	777.52	1,555.03	3,887.58	7,775.16
15	267.26	1,336.29	2,672.58	6,681.44	13,362.89
20	410.31	2,051.57	4,103.13	10,257.83	20,515.65

6% Interest

Years	$1	$5	$10	$25	$50
1	12.39	61.97	123.93	309.83	619.66
5	69.99	349.93	699.87	1,749.67	3,499.35
10	164.04	820.22	1,640.44	4,101.09	8,202.18
15	290.45	1,452.24	2,904.48	7,261.20	14,522.40
20	460.32	2,301.62	4,603.25	11,508.12	23,016.23

To illustrate, you might plan to save $10 monthly for 20 years prior to age 65. At a 6% semi-annual compound rate, you would have $4,603.25 at the end of that time. Each year your $4,603.25 would earn $280.34. You could withdraw approximately $23 each month while allowing your investment to remain intact. Or you might decide to withdraw your savings at the age of 65 and convert them to an annuity.

Annuity rates are currently quoted at $8 per $1,000 invested. With your savings of $4,603.25 you could purchase a lifetime monthly income of $36.80. If you need to double that amount, you should save $20 a month for the 20-year period.

Planning for Retirement Our illustration assumes that the retired couple chose to convert both life insurance and personal savings to annuities; it also assumes $427 social security benefits.

Monthly Retirement-Income Estimates

Social Security—Husband	$427.00
Life Insurance Converted to Annuity	73.58
Company Pension Plan	120.00
Personal Investments Converted to Annuity	36.80
Income Without Spouse	$657.38
Social Security—Spouse at 65	213.50
Total Monthly Income	$870.88

Because of extra exemptions at 65 and the standard deduction, a couple can receive $4,300 of income before owing any tax. Since social security payments are tax-exempt, and since the life-insurance annuity gets special tax treatment, the couple in our example would pay virtually no income tax on the $870.88 income.

To aid you in planning, you can use the same form and estimate your income. Two additional tables are provided, Table 9 and Table 10, which will help you to determine your savings goals.

Table 9: Value of $1.00 Invested

	Varying Compound Annual Interest Rates			
Year	4.0%	5.0%	6.0%	8.0%
1	$1.04000	$1.05000	$1.06000	$1.08000
5	1.21665	1.27628	1.33822	1.46932
10	1.48024	1.62889	1.79084	2.15892
15	1.80093	2.07892	2.39654	3.17216
20	2.19111	2.65328	3.20712	4.66094
25	2.66582	3.38633	4.29184	6.84844
30	3.24337	4.32191	5.74345	10.06260

Table 9 can be useful for planning what a specific sum of money saved now will be worth at a later date. For instance, $1.00 drawing interest at 6% will be worth $2.39654 in 15 years; $1,000 will have a value of $2,396.54. You can estimate what funds set aside now will be worth later when needed for college expenses or retirement.

Table 10 shows the amount you would have to deposit each month —in an account earning interest from day of deposit to day of withdrawal at 5¼% compounded daily—to accumulate the sum in the center column. The right side of Table 10 gives the amount you could withdraw from the account each month until the funds are depleted.

Table 10: Planned Savings and Withdrawals
(in Dollars)

Monthly Deposits					Monthly Withdrawals			
Years						Years		
5	10	15	20	Total	5	10	15	20
72.56	31.48	18.10	11.64	5,000	95.11	53.84	40.41	33.92
145.13	62.96	36.21	23.29	10,000	190.22	107.69	80.82	67.85
217.69	94.44	54.31	34.94	15,000	285.45	161.54	121.23	101.77
290.26	125.93	72.42	46.59	20,000	380.45	215.39	161.64	135.70
435.39	188.89	108.63	69.88	30,000	570.68	323.09	242.47	203.55
580.52	251.86	144.84	93.18	40,000	760.91	430.78	323.29	271.40
725.65	314.82	181.06	116.47	50,000	951.13	538.48	404.12	339.25

Table 10 can be very helpful in deciding how much you need to save monthly, *now,* so that specific sums can be accumulated. You also can learn how much those accumulated sums can produce in monthly withdrawals for a certain time period. For instance, you may estimate that college costs of $285 per month will be needed for a 5-year period, with 10 years to save before this need arises. You must save $94.44 each month to accumulate the $15,000 that is needed to provide $285.45 in monthly withdrawals for 5 years.

Is *family life cycle* a term you have considered? Most families manage resources on a paycheck-to-paycheck basis with little consideration of the changes in family needs in various periods of the family life cycle. Consider the illustration in this circle graph which

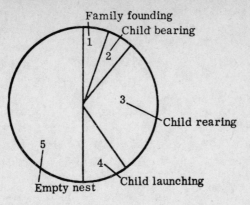

appeared in Today's Consumer, a workbook published by Home-making Research Laboratories of Tony, Wisconsin.

Needs during the empty-nest phase are certainly different from family needs during the first four stages. Long-range planning may prove most helpful. If the first 4 stages take 25 years, the married couple may be 50 years old. With some planning they could have paid off their 20-year home mortgage by the time their nest was empty. By continuing to invest for 15 more years that portion of the house payment which applied to interest and principal, their nest egg for age 65 could be substantial. Let's assume that their former house payment totaled $181.06 per month. By paying themselves now (making a monthly savings deposit) instead of the mortgage company, Table 10 reveals that in 15 years they will have accumulated $50,000. For the next 10 years they can plan on a monthly income of $538.48 (or $339.25 for 20 years). Such a plan would assume that they continue to live in the family home, which now may be more house than they need for the empty nest.

Where will *you* be in regard to income when your eggs hatch? Completion of a Monthly Retirement-Income Estimate form *now* could save many surprises later. God continually warns us not to *depend* upon annuities, social security, or dividends for our future. "We can make our plans, but the final outcome is in God's hands" (Proverbs 16:1).

DON'T FORGET WHO IS YOUR CHIEF INVESTMENT COUNSELOR!

11 Two Ways to Give After You Live

One-to-one is the statistic. The ratio has never changed. For every birth, there is a death!

Depending upon how long you live, you may reap the results of the careful planning of your nest eggs. You may also take steps *now* that will enable others to harvest the fruits of your provision after the time of your death. These steps involve your bodily organs and your earthly possessions.

Body Organs Last spring I attended the funeral of a Christian brother. Although my friend had not been a prominent civic worker or a top corporation executive, the large downtown church was full for his funeral. As I thought about my relationship with this man, I realized that he possessed some unusual giving qualities. His granddaughter had been born almost totally blind. Shortly after her birth, her parents had divorced. To fulfill his scriptural responsibilities, this grandfather began caring for the young girl. I have vivid memories of his bringing her to church, walking hand in hand with her, and fulfilling the responsibilities of parent to the girl. Whether assisting in the kindergarten or singing in the church choir, this fellow was always around giving himself to little details that others simply were not interested in handling. In my opinion, his servant attitude revealed his giving spirit.

When the minister delivered the eulogy, I was struck with the thought of how my friend gave *after* he lived as well as *while* he lived. For within a couple hours after his death his eyes were on the way to the Kansas Eye Bank. His hope was that they could be useful to someone who had no vision.

While he lived this man had taken the trouble to arrange for the gift of his eyes, with the expectation that someone else could see through them after he no longer needed those eyes. That action caused my wife and me to do some thinking about the stewardship of our own bodies at the time of our going to be with the Lord. Following are some of the things that I discovered; most of my information has been obtained from the National Kidney Foundation, a non-profit, voluntary health agency dedicated to finding the answer for the prevention, treatment, and cure of kidney diseases.

There are at least seventeen transplantable organs. It is now possible to replace a variety of malfunctioning human organs with increasing success. For example, in 1971 approximately six hundred organs were transplanted in Minnesota hospitals alone. Legislators in all states have passed the Uniform Anatomical Gift Act, making possible an organ-procurement program. The sample Uniform Donor Card and some questions and answers were provided by the National Kidney Foundation.

How are organs for transplantation obtained?

They are donated by individuals like yourself, with the donation going into effect at the time of death.

How can I become a donor?

Sign the card in the presence of two witnesses who also sign. Then carry the card on your person at all times. You will note that the card offers several options:

(a) indicates that you contribute any needed organs or parts

(b) restricts the donation to the organs or parts you specify

(c) gives your entire body for anatomical study

Is there an age requirement for donors?

Yes. Anyone 18 years of age or over and of sound mind may become a donor by signing the card. An individual under 18 years of age may become a donor if either parent or a legal guardian gives consent.

Do I have to register with some agency?

No. Your signed and witnessed donor card is all that is needed.

UNIFORM DONOR CARD

OF_____

Print or type name of donor

In the hope that I may help others, I hereby make this anatomical gift, if medically acceptable, to take effect upon my death. The words and marks below indicate my desires.

I give: (a) _____ any needed organs or parts

           (b) _____ only the following organs or parts

_____

Specify the organ(s) or part(s)

for the purposes of transplantation, therapy, medical research or education;

           (c) _____ my body for anatomical study if needed.

Limitations or
special wishes, if any : _____

Signed by the donor and the following two witnesses in the presence of each other:

_____   _____

Signature of Donor   Date of Birth of Donor

_____   _____

Date Signed   City & State

_____   _____

Witness   Witness

This is a legal document under the Uniform Anatomical Gift Act or similar laws.

For further information consult your physician or

KF National Kidney Foundation

Do I have to mention the organ donation in my will?

No. Your donor card is a kind of "pocket will" and is all you need. Mention it in your will if you wish. But obviously it's important to carry the card and also inform your family and physician to insure their cooperation.

Can I change my mind later?

Yes. Simply tear up the card. Nothing else is necessary.

Although I was challenged to consider this organ-donation idea over a year ago, I am probably like most of you reading this book.

I simply did nothing about it. Had I died within the year, all my organs would probably be resting now in a casket beneath a few feet of dirt. However, while I wrote this chapter, I took the Uniform Donor Card and discussed it with Marjean. We completed the cards in the presence of two witnesses. Now we carry them in our billfolds. I have also consulted my attorney and received the assurance that this is a valid and legal document under the Uniform Anatomical Gift Act in the state of Kansas.

Would you, too, like to know the joy of providing the gift of your organs to someone else who needs them after you die? If you need cards, write:

> National Kidney Foundation
> 116 East 27th Street
> New York, N.Y. 10016

You can see that the provision to give your organs after you die is a very specific way to give after you live. Another specific way concerns your will.

Your Will Do *you* have a will? If not, don't be too surprised to discover that you are among the majority of adults in the United States who have no will. A nationwide tax publication stated that seven out of eight people die without wills. Why is a will that important? What will happen to your property if you die without a will? The answer to that question will depend upon state laws which specify how your property is to be distributed. It will usually be divided in some way among the next of kin, but probably not the way you yourself would have liked to have had it divided. Because the court will appoint an administrator to distribute the property, there may be extra court expenses involved for the beneficiaries of your property. If there are no relatives, your property goes to the state.

Without a will, all of your property will be divided among relatives. None can be directed to any other beneficiary, such as to a church or charity. Not having a will is one way to make certain that you do not give after you live.

You may say, "I'm too young to have a will," or "I have so little, why should I have a will?"

Right after my second child was born, my insurance man talked to me about additional life insurance. He also asked if I had a will. I told him of course not, as I had hardly any property. Then he asked me another question, "If you and your wife are killed in some kind of accident, who will raise your children?" Since I couldn't answer him, I just shrugged my shoulders and gave him a silly look.

That evening I talked to Marjean about that situation. Did we want my parents to be responsible for raising the children, or did we want her parents to be responsible? Did we want her brother and sister-in-law, just newly married, to take over that responsibility, or would we choose one of our friends? These were tough questions, and we really hated to grapple with them. After all, weren't the chances of our being killed in a common situation very, very slim? But we couldn't dodge the issue. The chances were slight, but there was always that possibility. Also, we knew deep within our hearts that *we* wanted to dictate the guardianship of our children in case of a common disaster. We knew that we were in the best position to make that decision. And we knew that if we were killed without having made a guardianship decision, someone else would make it. It was this motivation, along with the urging of our insurance man and a recognition that this was the businesslike step to take, that motivated us to prepare our first will.

But maybe you do have a will. Does it provide for any giving out of your estate? If it does not, again you need not be surprised. My own experience is that most wills do not go beyond the almost automatic passing-it-on-to-closest-relatives stance. Even among large givers, few Christians give thought to other ways they can plan their estates and contribute significantly to the cause of Jesus Christ, both now and in the years to come.

Preparing a will helped me make some long-range plans and forced me to make some decisions about my basic giving philosophy. It also compelled me to take a good hard look at my own financial assets as well as my responsibilities.

My accountant showed me how to save significant amounts of taxes through increased giving from my estate. I established trusts to cover three possibilities for my family: my death with my wife surviving, my death without my wife surviving, and my death with none of my family surviving. Under each circumstance the trusts pro-

vided for gifts to specific Christian organizations after the purpose of
the trusts had been served. In other words, the federal government
actually encouraged me to give; if I took no steps, the federal government received the taxes. If I took the legal steps allowed under the
law, then I could determine which of the works of Christ would benefit from a portion of my estate, and estate taxes could be saved.

I can't begin to tell you the joy that I experienced when I finally
felt that I had my affairs and those of my wife in order through the
creation of wills and trusts to meet our responsibilities and our desires after death. But don't let me mislead you. People postpone
doing wills because procrastination is the easy thing to do. Most
people simply never get to their wills.

Creating a standard will is, of course, easier than choosing specifically those organizations which will receive portions of what you
elect to give. Preparing a thoughtful will which incorporated our giving philosophy was a difficult task, and it will be difficult for you, too.
But again, let me encourage you to take these steps so that you can
choose *now* how you want to give after you live.

You may not have a Christian attorney, or your Christian attorney
may have little experience in guiding you to effective giving. Never-
theless, there are places where you can receive help.

The chances are that you already have in mind one or two organizations which will be the recipients of your estate giving. Could it be
the particular denomination of your church? Is there some other
Christian organization that has had a significant ministry in your life
or in the lives of your family?

Most Christian organizations have a stewardship department with
professionally trained consultants to help you approach financial and
estate planning on a spiritual level. These services are usually offered
to you as a guide to stimulate your thinking. They are confidentially
done without charge or obligation. Usually the organizations make it
clear that they are not engaged in rendering legal or tax advisory
service. They may point out the need for an attorney in your own
state, since state laws govern wills, trusts, and charitable gifts made
in a contractual agreement. Representatives of these organizations
can be very helpful to you, because they have vast experience with
other Christians who desire to give after they live.

Let me suggest three possible sources for your consideration: the

stewardship department of your own denomination; Stewa
Department of World Vision, Inc., 919 West Huntington
Monrovia, CA 91016; and The Navigators, Planned Giving Director,
P.O. Box 1659, Colorado Springs, CO 80901.

In preparing my own will I discovered that in the ordinary will it
can be very difficult to allow the kind of flexibility that is desirable.
Let me give you an illustration. My mother is a widow whose primary
source of income is rent from a building she owns. The tenant of that
building is the collection agency that I own and operate. Her rent
plus her social security meet her current and foreseeable needs. As a
Christian, I recognize the responsibility I have to my mother as well
as to the other members of my family. If I were to die now, should I
leave my mother anything from my estate? The answer to that, of
course, is "it all depends." Someone else would be operating my business. The business may or may not succeed; the business may or may
not continue to rent the building from Mother; a new tenant may or
may not be found. If I provided a set sum of money for Mother in
my will, she might not need it. Then she would simply dispose of it
in her will at the point of her death, and it could be taxed again.

A trust agreement makes sense in this type of situation. I have
given the trustee power to use income from the trust, or to invade the
principal of the trust, for my mother's benefit. If she has a need, then
that need could be met from the trust. If she does not have a need,
then the trust will be disposed of, according to the trust agreement.

We also have an interest in the children of some of our brothers
and sisters in Christ. If we should die, we would like to provide for
the possibility of assisting with their educational expenses, if there is
a need. Again, in our written trust agreement, we have specified the
names of these families and charged the trustee with the responsibility
of determining whether there are needs to be met or not. If I die
before Marjean, then she can determine whether the needs exist or
not. In this way I will have the opportunity to continue my giving
after my living, the same as I would have done had I lived.

You will discover as you begin thinking through your own situation that there are a lot of difficult questions to answer. It makes a
lot of sense to grapple with those questions now and to arrive at a
desirable agreement, rather than to wait until you are faced with a
terminal illness, or even to leave such decisions to your mate to

make after a sudden death. The Bible says: "A prudent man foresees the difficulties ahead and prepares for them; the simpleton goes blindly on and suffers the consequences" (Proverbs 22:3). My high school Latin teacher often said, "A word to the wise is sufficient."

Recently I was visiting with a Christian about his will. He is a businessman of some means. I asked him if he had made any provision in his will for giving to the Lord's work after his death. He said no and then questioned me, "Since I tithe now on all my income, haven't I fulfilled my obligation to the Lord?" My answer was that it's not a matter of obligation but another giving opportunity. The Bible says we should give, "not grudgingly, or of necessity, for God loveth a cheerful giver" (*see* 2 Corinthians 9:7 KJV).

Unfortunately, preparing a will is not as easy as picking up the telephone, dialing your attorney, and saying, "Prepare a will for me." He can do that; but without facts and figures, he cannot prepare a will that would end up being a very personal document for you. Even if you already have a will, it may not accomplish your present objectives. The entire purpose of a will is to accomplish the desires of the maker.

To aid you in gathering information for your will, make a personal fact-finding survey of your financial affairs. The preparation of this survey will have two advantages for you: (1) It will force you to gather some information and make some decisions concerning the planning of your financial affairs. (2) It will provide the information necessary for you and your advisors to determine the most effective way to dispose of your property at the time of your death. The Navigators include a form titled "How to Help Your Attorney" in their workbook *Planning a Will*.

Do you remember that I told you making a will would not be easy? But as Christians, who wants the easy way? Serving the Lord often means taking the harder path. It is certainly the desire of my life that I live to the glory of God.

Paul also tells us: "however, be sure that everything is done properly in a good and orderly way" (1 Corinthians 14:40). Having a will which includes the stewardship of my possessions, after I no longer need them, is one way I can give glory to God after I live and present a witness to others.

12   But God!

For several years after I became a Christian, I tried to give more money to the Lord. I can't tell you what a relief it was when I finally took the plunge and decided to give a tenth of my gross income to the Lord's work.

My wife and I had been in a home Bible-study group for several months. One night the thrust of the discussion centered around trusting versus trying. There seems to be a fine line between trying so hard to do something and trusting the Lord to do it for you. We knew that we wanted to trust the Lord for every area of our lives. There was a gnawing suspicion that trying to give Him a little more money each year was not really trusting Him to meet all of our needs. Somehow I was directed by the Scriptures that if I was unwilling to give God at least 10% of my total income, then I really was not trusting Him at all. Proverbs 3:4–6 has been a great help in this area. The Living Bible says, "If you want favor with both God and man, and a reputation for good judgment and common sense, then trust the Lord completely; don't ever trust yourself. In everything you do, put God first, and he will direct you and crown your efforts with success." It has been exciting to trust Him more and more, and the percentage of our income that is given to the Lord's work has increased in proportion to our trust in Him.

Because I am so practical, I developed a very unscriptural habit of giving. From time to time preachers had told me in sermons that a person was to give in proportion as he received his income. This seemed like a ridiculous waste of checks, time, and energy to me. Consequently, I made my pledge and with one grand swoop sent a check for all of it at the end of the year. Such action gave me the added security that if I had had a bad year, then I might just postpone payment of my pledge until the next year. During those days I was also considering whether I needed the tax deduction more in the current year, or whether I should postpone the gift until the first of the new year in order to have the deduction mean the most to me. There was also the element of pride involved, since I reasoned that not everyone in the church would have the kind of discipline that I had and be able to plunk down an entire church pledge in one fell swoop.

But God!

But God zapped me with His Word again. "On every Lord's Day each of you should put aside something from what you have earned during the week, and use it for this offering. The amount depends on how much the Lord has helped you earn. Don't wait until I get there and then try to collect it all at once" (1 Corinthians 16:2). God's Word made it clear that I was to give regularly in proportion to my income.

The practical application of this lesson was to establish a separate bank account for our giving. Each payday our giving amount is automatically set aside from our income and deposited into the *giving account*. Checks are specially printed in a different color from our usual spending checks. We even have the fish symbol on the checks as a witness to all who receive them. Whenever extra income arrives, the giving percentage is set aside in the giving account.

Giving God the first part of all my income is a specific way that I can put Him first in my life. "The purpose of tithing is to teach you always to put God first in your lives" (*see* Deuteronomy 14:23). One of my friends says that tithing *was not instituted by God to raise money* but to train children.

Have you experienced the joy that comes from taking that initial step of establishing the tithe as a regular reminder that it all belongs to God?

Consider another advantage of the separate giving account. Most taxpayers do not claim charitable contributions at the level of anything like 10% or more of their gross income. In talking to other tithers I have found that most all of them have had their statements audited by the Internal Revenue Service. In each case the primary focus of the audit was on the charitable contributions. My own mother who is a tither was summoned recently by the Internal Revenue Service to produce evidence of her charitable contributions. I had the same experience a few months later. The separate checkbook made our audits a pleasant experience.

The discovery that there can be more to giving than simply sending a check has been a real blessing to us. A couple of years ago a young man and his wife stopped by our house en route to their new campus ministry at a state university. We had heard the young man's testimony a few months earlier. When given the opportunity we were delighted to have a financial part in their ministry. When he explained their financial needs, he said that his support had already reached a level of so many hundred dollars per month. Then he shared his goal with us. Our response was to tell him that we would like to be involved for a specific amount each month. After we had prayer with them and they left, my wife and I agreed that we should also send some words of encouragement with our monthly check.

Since that time we have developed a personal involvement with the couple. They have stayed in our home several times, and we have shared the hospitality of their home. Seldom has a month gone by in which we have not communicated with each other by letter or telephone. Whenever we have a special prayer request, we advise them of it, knowing that they will pray faithfully. The blessings we have received have far exceeded the small monthly gift we have given.

My business is to try to collect bills that people did not pay to their creditors. A collection agency is really in the salvage business. When a creditor gives up trying to collect his own accounts, he turns them over to a collection agency. Our job is to locate the people who owe the money and sell them on the idea of paying the bill. We are essentially issuing calls to responsibility. I feel that people should keep the promises they make to other people about money. Otherwise, they lose some self-respect and carry around a load of guilt.

A military credit union sent us an account to collect in the amount of $285. The airman who owed the note had been discharged from the Air Force for car theft and for being AWOL. His whereabouts were unknown. For several months one of my employees followed his trail all over the United States. The car on which the money was owed was sold; and the young man was involved in drugs.

But God!

But God got hold of this fellow through a friend. We located him in a Teen Challenge center in Texas. The director of the center told us that the former airman was there in his first few weeks as a Christian. He was in the process of withdrawing from drugs and was beginning a study of God's Word. The director explained very carefully that the new convert had no money, was receiving no income, and would not be able to work for several months.

Imagine our surprise a few weeks later when we received a letter from the debtor along with a check for $135. His letter said, "The Lord has provided this money to pay on my debt. As soon as He provides more, I will send it."

I don't know what kind of image you have of a bill collector or what kind of experience you may have had with one. But the collector in my office who received this letter excitedly shared it with me. Could it be that God had changed the direction of this young man's life? We remembered, "If anyone is in Christ, he is a new creation." How could we be an encouragement to him? We sent his receipt and a contribution to Teen Challenge. We wrote a note of encouragement to the fellow for facing the responsibility of paying his debt.

Within a few days he wrote to our office. Thus began a regular correspondence between him and our own family. It has been a thrill to watch him grow in Christ. He has graduated from two Teen Challenge programs. His debt to the credit union is completely paid as well as other debts that he made during his wild sprees. He is now in a Bible college training to be a full-time worker with Teen Challenge.

The first Christmas after we corresponded with him, we had the pleasure of having him in our home for a few days. Through a simple act of giving, God has built a meaningful relationship and Christian fellowship that will extend into eternity. Do you see what I mean about fantastic opportunities for giving?

People frequently ask whether all my giving is done through my local church. In my case, the answer to that is no. Approximately 50% of my giving supports ministries beyond the local church. We enjoy supporting individuals who have a ministry in which we can be involved. Examples include Young Life leaders, Navigator representatives, Campus Crusade workers, World Impact ghetto workers, and college workers such as those with the Baptist Student Union.

For each of these individual ministries we have a small card. Each morning at our breakfast table we pray for the person on the top card of the group. We pray for him, his family, and the ministry in which he is involved. A large world map next to our breakfast table enables us to use pins for visual evidence of where these ministries are taking place. As we give, we feel a responsibility to pray for those with whom we are involved.

One of the great discoveries of my life was a "spiritual vacation." For years I had flown a small airplane all over the United States so that my family might enjoy the tourist attractions of this great country. Most of the time we arrived back home exhausted and broke. I usually called these trips *vacation* because I heard once that "a vacation is what you take when you can't take what you're taking any longer." But I hardly felt renewed spiritually or restored physically.

But God!

But God led us to a summer conference at the Navigator headquarters in Colorado Springs. If you have not experienced the true refreshment that comes from a week in Christian fellowship, Bible study, and prayer, you will not understand what I am talking about. Since our first taste of a spiritual vacation, we have not had a year when we did not return to some kind of a Christian learning experience for a deeper feeding from God's Word.

Such spiritual vacations may be a legitimate income-tax deduction. Since I am not qualified to provide tax counsel, I suggest that you check with your tax advisor before claiming a deduction for any trip. Many trips have been training experiences for my wife and me, and our training has then been used in service to our local church congregation. My CPA has advised me that the use of such training usually qualifies a trip for a tax deduction. The Internal Revenue Service agreed with me on my last audit. (But don't forget to keep good records.)

Giving beyond the tithe has been a joy for us. Have you experienced this joy in your own life, or are you holding out on God and trusting in your money? *Your checkbook will indicate whether you are really trusting God or trusting your money*. The Prophet Malachi clearly shows that there is a difference in our lives according to the way we rob God or give to Him.

> "Will a man rob God? Surely not! And yet you have robbed me.
> " 'What do you mean? When did we ever rob you?'
> "You have robbed me of the tithes and offerings due to me. And so the awesome curse of God is cursing you, for your whole nation has been robbing me. Bring all the tithes into the storehouse so that there will be food enough in my Temple; if you do, I will open up the windows of heaven for you and pour out a blessing so great you won't have room enough to take it in! Try it! Let me prove it to you!"
>
> Malachi 3:8–10

This is the Lord's message to the people of Israel, given through the prophet. God seems to be saying about generous and joyful giving:

TRY IT, YOU'LL LIKE IT!

13 Rent? Buy?

You may have heard about the man who was asked, "Do you have trouble making decisions?" His reply was a slow but definite, "Well, yes and no." *Your* answer to the question as to whether to rent or to buy a place to live will be a sharp, "It all depends."

The Bible counsels us to proceed carefully before making major financial commitments. "It is dangerous and sinful to rush into the unknown" (Proverbs 19:2).

Americans have been rushing into the unknown in home buying ever since the end of World War II. Owning your own home has been the dream of most young couples. The big justification question is: "Why pay all that rent and end up with nothing?" Following this question comes the positive justification: "You might as well be buying your home as pouring all that rent down the drain."

Mortgage companies have made homeownership easier by extending the length of mortgages from 20 to 25, and now, to 30 years. As the length of time has been extended, the percentage of down payment required has been reduced. The result, of course, is a higher mortgage over a longer period of time—all of which means vastly more interest paid than with the shorter term, smaller mortgages. Table 11 shows the effect of the length of term on the monthly payment and the amount of interest paid.

Some startling facts are revealed by the table. The monthly payment for a 20-year mortgage is $269.92; for 30 years the payment is $241.39. The 30-year mortgage payment is $28.53 a month (or

Table 11: Effects of Mortgage Term on Mortgage Costs

Mortgage: $30,000   Interest Rate: 9%

Mortgage Term	Monthly Payment	Total Payment	Total Interest	Interest as % of Principal
15 years	$304.28	$54,770	$24,770	83
20 years	269.92	64,781	34,781	116
25 years	251.76	75,528	45,528	152
30 years	241.39	86,895	56,895	190

10.5%) less than the 20-year payment. The difference in interest cost between a 30-year and a 20-year mortgage is a whopping $22,114 (or 63.6% more) for the longer mortgage. However, I'm told by savings-and-loan executives that approximately 95% of all home loans are being made for the more costly 30-year periods.

Careful analysis of such facts allows you the opportunity to understand the costs involved in such decisions as size of monthly payments and length and size of mortgage. For instance, the $30,000 mortgage for a 20-year term will have these conditions and results: (a) a monthly payment of $269.92; (b) the payment is $28.53 higher than the $241.39 monthly required for a 30-year loan; and (c) the additional $28.53 a month paid the first 20 years will add up to $6,847 more than would have been paid in that period, if the 30-year loan had been chosen.

What has the extra $6,847 in payments the first 20 years produced? The homeowner now has a debt-free home and avoids 10 years of monthly payments of $241.39—a total of $28,967 (10 × 12 × $241.39).

The shorter mortgage has saved you $22,120 ($28,967 − $6,847). That's a fantastic result for squeezing out an extra $28.53 monthly for those first 20 years! And the absence of that large, monthly house payment could be extremely significant to you 20 years from now.

If you can't work your budget to squeeze out the extra $28.53 each month and still want the 20-year loan, you could consider a less expensive home and a smaller mortgage. Buying a $3,000 less costly house and mortgage would lower monthly payments by $26.99 on the 20-year mortgage.

Table 12: Distribution of Mortgage Payments
(Mortgage $30,000: Interest 9%)

Year	Payment on Interest	Payment on Principal	Balance Due	Equity in Mortgage
1	$ 2,691.69	$ 204.99	$29,795.01	$ 204.99
2	2,672.46	224.22	29,570.79	429.21
3	2,651.42	245.26	29,325.53	674.47
4	2,628.42	268.26	29,057.27	942.73
5	2,603.25	293.43	28,763.84	1,236.16
6	2,575.72	320.96	28,442.88	1,557.12
7	2,545.60	351.08	28,091.80	1,908.20
8	2,512.69	383.99	27,707.81	2,292.19
9	2,476.66	420.02	27,287.79	2,712.21
10	2,437.26	459.42	26,828.37	3,171.63
11	2,394.16	502.52	26,325.85	3,674.15
12	2,347.01	549.67	25,776.18	4,223.82
13	2,295.45	601.23	25,174.95	4,825.05
14	2,239.05	657.63	24,517.32	5,482.68
15	2,177.37	719.31	23,798.01	6,201.99
16	2,109.90	786.78	23,011.23	6,988.77
17	2,036.10	860.58	22,150.65	7,849.35
18	1,955.36	941.32	21,209.33	8,790.67
19	1,867.05	1,029.63	20,179.70	9,820.30
20	1,770.46	1,126.22	19,053.48	10,946.52
21	1,664.81	1,231.87	17,821.61	12,178.39
22	1,549.25	1,347.43	16,474.18	13,525.82
23	1,422.86	1,473.82	15,000.36	14,999.64
24	1,284.60	1,612.08	13,388.28	16,611.72
25	1,133.39	1,763.29	11,624.99	18,375.01
26	967.99	1,928.69	9,696.30	20,303.70
27	787.06	2,109.62	7,586.68	22,413.32
28	589.17	2,307.51	5,279.17	24,720.83
29	372.70	2,523.98	2,755.19	27,244.81
30	135.93	2,755.19	. . . .	30,000.00
Total	$56,894.84	$30,000.00		

Total Payments on
Interest and Principal $86,894.84

Another factor to consider when buying a home is the probable length of time you plan to live there. You may be surprised to learn how little equity you build during the first few years with those large monthly payments. Table 12 shows the schedule on a $30,000, 9% mortgage for 30 years. The monthly payment is $241.39—a total of $2,896.68 annually.

The equity at the end of the first year is only $204.99, at the end of 7 years only $1,908.20. By the end of 7 years you've paid 84 monthly payments totaling $20,276.76! It is not until you have paid 23 years, or 77% of the time of your mortgage, that your equity in the mortgage is up to $15,000—50% of the mortgage. Your interest costs through the twenty-third year have totaled $51,624.

Since the average length of time Americans own a home is seven years, those starting with new long-term mortgages do not have much equity to "play with" when they sell. Unless the house has appreciated substantially in value, they might actually be fortunate to escape the sale, after real-estate commissions, with any money at all. That's the same as paying rent—but with a lot more headaches.

You can develop figures for your own consideration when you contemplate a long-term mortgage.

Mortgage-Term Comparisons

Amount of Mortgage	$ _____		Interest Rate _____
Mortgage Term	Monthly Payment	Total Payment	Total Interest
20 years	_____	_____	_____
25 years	_____	_____	_____
30 years	_____	_____	_____
Mortgage Schedule	Balance due end of:		

Mortgage Term	5 years	10 years	15 years	20 years	25 years	30 years
20 years	____	____	____	____	____	____
25 years	____	____	____	____	____	____
30 years	____	____	____	____	____	____
Equity in Home	Subtract balance due from mortgage amount and add amount of down payment.					

Mortgage Term	5 years	10 years	15 years	20 years	25 years	30 years
20 years	____	____	____	____	____	____
25 years	____	____	____	____	____	____
30 years	____	____	____	____	____	____

To help you estimate the costs of homeownership the following form is provided.

Annual Cost of a Home

A. Average Annual Interest (on mortgage and interest income you are foregoing at _____%)
To figure, multiply rate of interest by purchase price _____
B. Taxes—2.5% cost of home _____
C. Maintenance—2% cost of home _____
D. Insurance—½ of 1% cost of home _____
E. Total Annual Cost _____
F. Equivalent Monthly Rent (E ÷ 12) _____

A rule of thumb for homeownership is that the monthly costs usually approximate 1.2% of the purchase price. Note that those costs only include the amounts listed on the Annual Cost of a Home form. They exclude the expenses of *living* in a house such as utilities, decorations, small repairs and supplies. Don't forget the potential costs of such items as drapes, carpets, built-in appliances, and shrubs, all of which can add up to many thousands of dollars for a new house or just as much for replacement in an older home.

To calculate your own costs and make comparisons between your present home or apartment and a different home or apartment use the Cost of Homeownership form, page 112. You will want to consider that the equity you hold in the house (or the down payment in the case of a newly purchased house) would yield a return if invested elsewhere. If the house will not appreciate in value at a level as high as alternate current yields, you may want to reflect that factor in the cost of ownership. If you choose an apartment you will presumably have these funds to place in savings, annuities, or other investments.

At interest rates of 6 years ago a friend of mine borrowed $35,000 on a home he purchased for $39,500. He had a monthly payment of $409, including principal, interest, taxes, and insurance. Would you believe that, after paying on his house for 6 years (72 payments), his 30-year mortgage still had a balance due of $33,009? With 72 payments the principal had been reduced by $1,991 or a mere 5.7%.

Cost of Homeownership

	Home A	Home B	Apartment
Home Cost (or Value)	$_____	$_____	
Annual Costs			
Estimated Annual Interest	_____	_____	
Adjustment for Alternative Use of Equity Money	_____	_____	
Real Estate Taxes	_____	_____	
Maintenance & Repairs *	_____	_____	
Utilities			
(a) Electricity	_____	_____	_____
(b) Water & Sewer	_____	_____	_____
(c) Gas	_____	_____	_____
(d) Trash	_____	_____	_____
(e) Other	_____	_____	_____
Remodeling	_____	_____	
Other	_____	_____	_____
Apartment Rent			_____
Total	==========	==========	==========

* Be sure to estimate costs for repairs and replacement for such items as built-in appliances; service contracts on furnace and air conditioning; painting; repairs on roof, gutters, plumbing, electrical systems, driveway, and walks; lawn care and shrubs. Don't forget to count on those one-time costs when you buy the home. Closing costs usually run about 2% of the loan or higher.

That's less than $28 per month increase in the equity in his house— hardly a sizeable investment.

His house sold in late 1974, after a period of rapid real-estate inflation, for $66,500. How did he come out on his investment in a house? Fabulously!

Sales price	$66,500
Less real-estate commission (6%)	3,990
Net from sale	$62,510

Less amount of original down payment	4,500
Less cost of improvements	4,000
	$54,010
Less loan due	33,009
Gain on sale of house	$21,001
Gain per month	$291.68

There are some potential catches to that profit.

If he does not buy another house for at least what he netted from the one he sold, there is the matter of capital-gains tax to be paid. The taxable gain has already been reduced by the amount he invested in capital improvements in the house (a good case for keeping accurate records).

The chances are, though, if your house shows rapid appreciation for the time you live in it, your sale would net you some profit. And that's better than paying rent. Consider, too, your interest charges are tax-deductible.

But what if the house did not appreciate? A lot of factors are involved for a house to increase in value. I built my first house in 1957 in a very nice area of Wichita. When it sold ten years later, I didn't profit a dollar on it, even though I received a fair market price at that time. Style, location, the community economy, cost of borrowing money, and timing—all play a part in whether your house sells at a gain or a loss on your investment.

There are many benefits to apartment living. You should consider the pros and cons yourself before plunging into a long-term mortgage on a home of your own. Apartments are renting for approximately 30¢ per month per square foot. A monthly rent of $400 at 30¢ a square foot would provide the same apartment space as a house of 1,333 square feet. Here are some advantages and disadvantages of living in the apartment.

Advantages of Apartment

Fixed monthly expense
Freedom from responsibilities of homeownership
No unexpected repairs or maintenance

Minimum time involved in upkeep
Probable use of a swimming pool, clubhouse, and sauna
No funds invested
No chance of loss on sale
No permanent commitment
Security of near neighbors during absence and presence

Disadvantages of Apartment

Builds no financial equity
No tax deductions
Less privacy
Less solitude outside
Unable to decorate as you please
Rents can be increased
Lease entanglements
No possible gain on sale
Maintenance and upkeep may be less than desired
No pride in ownership

Depending upon your own likes and dislikes, you may consider some advantages listed as disadvantages in your own case. The couple who doesn't enjoy yard work, do-it-yourself projects, and home decorating may find the apartment especially appealing. But a creative couple whose hobby is fixing things up may be very frustrated in an apartment.

Whether you rent or buy, a place to live will be one of the major financial commitments you make. Housing expenses will usually account for 25% to 30% of your gross income. A person buying a $30,000 house with a 95%, 30-year loan will pay $1,500 down. At today's interest rates of 9.5% the monthly payment of principal and interest will total $239.65. That's a 30-year payment total of $86,274; interest and principal costs, plus down payment, total $87,774. Taxes, over a 30-year period, would add at least $22,500 more; insurance, $4,500; and maintenance, $18,000. (The house is assumed to hold its value of $30,000 with taxes figured at

2.5%, insurance at 0.5%, and maintenance at 2%.) That's a grand total of $132,774. If this is 25% of your gross income during the 30 years, you will need to earn over one-half million dollars ($531,096 or $17,703 annually) to support your $30,000 house.

How can you know what price house is right for your family? This is not an easy question to answer. Two rules of thumb can be used as guides. First, the price of the house you buy today should not exceed 1.8 times your annual income. The second guide is that your total housing costs should not exceed 30% of your gross income. Using the figures for the house above, both rules can be illustrated, since they are mutually related to each other.

To buy a $30,000 home (using 1.8 times the gross annual income as a guide) requires yearly earnings of $16,667 ($30,000 ÷ 1.8). The maximum recommended cost of a house for a buyer with an annual income of $16,667 is $30,000.

Using our second guide, that housing costs should not exceed 30% of gross income, we can see the relationship between the two guides. Here are the monthly and annual costs for the $30,000 house, purchased with a $1,500 down payment and a 30-year 9.5% loan.

Total Housing Costs

	Monthly	Annually
Principal & Interest	$239.65	$2,875.80
Taxes (2.5%)	62.50	750.00
Insurance (0.5%)	12.50	150.00
Maintenance (2%)	50.00	600.00
Utilities	58.00	696.00
Totals	$422.65	$5,071.80

Total housing costs of $5,072 are near to 30.4% of the $16,667 gross annual income. To buy a more costly home would increase annual costs, throw the home-cost figure above 30%, and make a balanced budget extremely difficult, if not impossible. Keep in mind that the 30% figure should be considered as a *top* limit. The higher the annual income, the easier it usually is to spend close to the 30% on housing. But for gross incomes much below the $16,667 level, the housing costs would need to be nearer to the 25% figure, and less if possible.

Not only is the place you choose to live a major financial involvement, but also your living situation plays a major role in your lifestyle and that of your family. Much of your life revolves around the home. Most of your meals are shared there. An attitude of delight and joy about the place you call *home* should exert a positive influence on the lives of you and your family.

What are the spiritual principles to follow in making such an important decision? They are:

> Get the facts.
> Seek godly counsel.
> Seek God's counsel.

Get the Facts.　The purchase of your home may be the largest financial transaction you ever make. The real-estate agent has a specific vested interest in the transaction—his commission. No sale, no commission. Do not expect the realtor to present you with all the gory details about interest, closing costs, and length of mortgages. That's your responsibility. The Bible has a good warning for you: "Only a simpleton believes what he is told! A prudent man checks to see where he is going" (Proverbs 14:15). God's counsel is to learn all you can about the cost and the terms. Especially be realistic in comparing all the costs of the particular house you're interested in with your ability to pay such costs.

An excellent way to shop for a house is to determine ahead of time exactly what you want and figure out a top limit to your down payment and your monthly payment. No matter how excited you become about a particular house, if it does not contain all you want in a house, or if it will require more than your limits of down payment and monthly payments, then you should keep praying and looking for another place.

My wife and I had looked at houses for two or three years without ever finding exactly what we thought we wanted. Our financial limits had also been established. Since we had not found *the house* in such a length of time, we decided that we might not be clear about what we wanted.

Early in July we made a room-by-room list of what we desired inside a house. We listed overall qualifications such as a quiet street, a patio, and some nice-sized trees. We even mentioned the exterior since we wanted it to be as free of maintenance as possible. We also determined that we wanted to remain in our same neighborhood.

In less than three weeks a realtor called for us to come to see a certain house. We had looked at that house earlier in June and rejected it as undesirable because of a few things we didn't like. But we agreed to look again.

Armed with our list, we went through the house. We were amazed to see how it met every one of our written requirements, room by room. Now, the two things we didn't like looked very small in comparison to the way the place met our stated needs.

However, the price was too much. The total sales price exceeded our maximum by about $8,000. We explained this to the realtor. To our surprise, she suggested that we present an offer based on what we could comfortably pay. Incidentally, we had assured her that, at that price, we could come up with the sizeable amount of cash that was necessary to make the purchase without obtaining a new loan. To our great surprise, the owner readily accepted our offer. We were mowing the lawn of our new home five days after we had gone to look at it this time. We had exactly what we wanted according to our written list. Also, we had bought it at a figure compatible with our written limits.

Seek Godly Counsel. One reason we seek godly counsel is that the Bible tells us not to seek ungodly counsel. "Blessed is the man that walketh not in the counsel of the ungodly, nor standeth in the way of sinners, nor sitteth in the seat of the scornful" (Psalms 1:1 KJV). Another reason to seek godly counsel is found in Proverbs 10:21: "A godly man gives good advice . . . ."

Seek God's Counsel. His counsel is available for the asking. Of all the fantastic promises in the Bible I can't think of any that excite me more than those promising God's guidance. A few of those promises are these:

> I will bless the Lord who counsels me; he gives me wisdom in the night. He tells me what to do.
>
> Psalms 16:7

He shows how to distinguish right from wrong, how to find the right decision every time.

Proverbs 2:9

"Listen to my counsel—oh, don't refuse it—and be wise."

Proverbs 8:33

Why do so many Christians fail to obtain the facts, seek godly counsel, and ask the Lord's direction before taking major financial steps? My answer is that they simply don't want any facts or any person or even the Lord to stop them from doing what they want to do.

Have you noticed in yourself or in others how excited most people get when they spend money? The larger the purchase, the more excitement. There is a fine line of thinking in any purchase where the prospective buyer envisions owning the item. When this stage is reached, the time for sound thinking is usually passed. Emotions take over. The plunge is made. The financial transaction is consummated. Frequently the facts about costs are swept aside completely in the excitement of making the purchase.

Beware of such emotionalism. Before moving to our present house, we found one other home that we liked. I offered the owner the amount that we could afford, which was well under his asking price; the owner refused the offer. The problem was that Marjean had already emotionally moved into the house, arranged the furniture, and entertained our first guests. It was a real shock to her to realize that we were not moving into that house!

What should you do about a house? That all depends upon:

> Your requirements
> The real-estate market
> Interest rates
> The right house
> Counsel
> The facts
> Your financial situation
> God's guidance

To find the answer, claim the Bible's telephone verse, Jeremiah 33:3: "Call unto me, and I will answer thee, and shew thee great and mighty things, which thou knowest not" (KJV).

14 The Best Deal I Ever Made

Money was involved in the best deal I ever made.

In the summer of 1949 I decided to hitchhike from Dallas, where I was attending college, back to my hometown in Kansas. Hitchhiking was a money-saving method. A friend took me up to the north edge of Dallas, and I started out the process. The first ride only took me to Denton, Texas. As I got out of the car, a real Texas summer thunderstorm hit, and I hurriedly took shelter for a couple hours.

After the storm cleared, I headed for the north end of town where I began holding out my thumb again. The first car that stopped was a Model A Ford. Since I was obviously trying to get a ride, I couldn't figure out any way to tell the man I didn't want to get into his old car. Reluctantly I climbed inside.

To this day I still have a vivid memory of that scene. We were driving down the road with the wind roaring in all the openings of that ancient black auto. Next to me sat a large man with a black beard, dressed in a black suit. On the seat beside us was a thick, black Bible. I don't remember any of the conversation that day except for one question the fellow shouted at me over the noise of the car, "Brother, are you a Christian?"

Confidently I answered, "I sure am." Then I explained further, "I've gone to Sunday school and church all my life. I'm attending a Christian college, and I'm rooming with a young man who's studying to be a preacher." After all that, surely the old man believed that I was a Christian. At least if he didn't, I did!

Twelve years later one of the ministers in the church where I belonged asked if my wife and I would accept a scholarship to attend a week-long retreat in another city. By this time I had been president of a Sunday-school class, held several positions in the church, and even assisted my wife in teaching Sunday school. Attending a retreat had never occurred to me; however, the minister said there was some scholarship money available, and that our way would be paid. Oh, how money does talk. The idea of going away to spend a week on a beautiful college campus—at someone else's expense—appealed to me.

While attending this retreat my wife and I noticed that the others there seemed to have a different spirit than we had experienced in church. They had a love for each other which was expressed openly in various ways. They carried their Bibles around and were not only reading them, but they seemed to be excited about what they read. During the week we met in small prayer groups, and I experienced moments of prayer such as I had never known. Each morning began with a period of silence in which the 150 participants sat under the cottonwood trees reading their Bibles. At the end of 45 minutes people began to stand up and indicate "what the Lord told them" as they had read their Bibles that morning. I had been reading my Bible, too, but I was dumbfounded to hear that God had actually spoken to others as they read. Such was certainly not my experience.

Sometime during the week that old man's question came back to me. It was the first time that I had thought about it since he had asked it twelve years earlier. The question kept echoing, "Brother, are you a Christian? Brother, are you a Christian? Brother, are you a Christian?" The answer was clear. Now I knew that sitting in church would not make me a Christian any more than spending all my time in a chicken house would make me a chicken. I was hungry to come into a loving, personal relationship with Jesus Christ.

During the final night of the retreat, the minister preached on this text from Revelation: "Behold, I stand at the door and knock; if any one hears my voice and opens the door, I will come in to him and eat with him, and he with me" (3:20 RSV). The minister explained the picture that hung in the front of the sanctuary—a painting of Jesus standing and knocking at a door. The door represented the heart of a person. There was no latch on the outside of the door. He said that Jesus was a gentleman and would not force Himself into anyone's life. He further explained that Christ came into a life when the person on the inside opened the door and invited Him in.

The minister issued an invitation to anyone who had heard the Lord Jesus Christ knocking on the door of his heart and wanted to ask Him to come in. As he invited those to come forward who wanted to make that decision, I stood up. At the same time Marjean stood and took my hand. Together we walked down the aisle, but individually we invited Christ to come into our lives.

As we returned home from that retreat, we talked about various areas of our lives. Once again money reared its head. We had not driven many miles before I confessed to my wife the selfish attitude I had had concerning the college scholarship given to me by my national church organization which I had not yet chosen to repay. Previously, it had been sufficient for me to rationalize that, after all, it was a scholarship earned because of my superior high-school grades. The national church organization had sent letters reminding me that the scholarship did not carry a legal obligation, but it did carry a moral agreement to repay. Those letters usually motivated me to an annual contribution of some $25, which wouldn't even cover the interest on the $1,600 that had been furnished for my college education. But God spoke clearly to me as a new Christian. On that trip home we resolved to pay back every dollar of that scholarship so that other youngsters could have the same opportunity I had had.

Our giving did increase substantially during the years immediately after we became Christians. It was not until I began a regular study and meditation on God's Word, however, that I was led to the position to tithe as well as give additional offerings. The joy of giving is a real blessing to us now.

Another blessing has been the sharing of our giving with our two daughters. It has been a delight to train them in giving as well as in the area of stewardship of their time and possessions. The Bible says: "Train up a child in the way he should go . . ." (Proverbs 22:6 RSV). I believe that part of that training includes faithfulness in whatever money the child has.

You can see that money was involved in the best deal that I ever made. Nothing I know compares with the joy of knowing Jesus Christ personally. Nothing I know compares with the privilege of sharing the first minutes of each day with Him. Nothing I know equals the excitement and amazement that comes from the super ways He answers my prayers. Nothing I know compares with the uncanny way God has of zapping me with His Word in my areas of weakness. Nothing I know compares to the thrill of my obedience to His commandments. When He says, "This is the way, walk ye in it" (*see* Isaiah 30:21 KJV), and I do it, there is a peace and a joy that transcends anything money can ever buy.

How about you? Have you made the best deal of your life? Have you invited the Lord Jesus Christ to come into your heart forever?

To experience the security of His Eternal Presence, why not close your eyes wherever you are now and invite Christ to come into your life? You can repeat this simple prayer:

> Lord Jesus, I acknowledge that I have heard You knocking at the door of my heart. I now invite You to come into my life. Thank You for being so patient with me, and thank You for giving me the gift right now of eternal life with You. Amen.

Welcome to God's forever family, Brother! You are now one of all God's children, and if money has been talking to you the way it did to me, you probably have some things to set in order with what God has allowed you to have.

And Brother, if you were already a Christian and have read through this book, it is my prayer that God has given you some new insights and some practical aids so that you can become less faithful to unrighteous mammon and receive increased responsibilities in the true riches.

Are there portions of your financial life that need correction? Don't put it off. Those areas in which you are holding back are cancers. Conversely, in every area in which you are obedient, you can expect greater and greater blessings. Revelation 22:11 is a tremendous challenge for each of us, not only in areas of financial responsibility, but also in every area of our lives. The Living Bible states it this way: "And when that time comes, all doing wrong will do it more and more; the vile will become more vile; good men will be better; those who are holy will continue on in greater holiness."

The goal for our money as well as for every area of our lives is to continue on in greater holiness. To continue in holiness we must continue in His Word. As Jesus said, "If you continue in my word, you are truly my disciples, and you will know the truth, and the truth will make you free" (*see* John 8:31, 32 RSV). I discovered that Jesus is "the Way, and the Truth, and the Life" just as He said (*see* John 14:6). I've also discovered that the Scriptures are the best financial handbook I've ever found.

Scriptural References on Selected Financial Topics

This list provides scriptural references for a variety of subjects dealing with money and possessions. Your personal application of these biblical principles could lead you to new freedom with your finances. Many of these verses, applied to my own life, have rewarded me with a new joy in the sharing, saving, and spending of what God has entrusted to me. All Scriptures are from The Living Bible unless otherwise noted.

Be Content   Joshua 7:7; Luke 3:14 NEB; 2 Corinthians 6:10; Philippians 4:11, 12; 1 Timothy 6:6–10 PHILLIPS; Hebrews 13:5 RSV.

Budgeting   Proverbs 22:3; 24:3, 4; 27:12; Luke 14:28–30.

Child Training   Proverbs 22:6 RSV; Ephesians 6:4 RSV.

Cosigner   Proverbs 6:1–5; 11:15; 17:18; 20:16; 22:26, 27:13.

Counsel   Psalms 1:1 KJV; 16:7; Proverbs 2:9; 8:33; 10:21; 15:22 RSV; Jeremiah 33:3 KJV.

Debt   Psalms 37:21; Proverbs 1:17, 18; 3:27, 28; 22:7; Romans 13:8 PHILLIPS.

Discipline   Matthew 7:13, 14 RSV; Luke 9:51; 2 Corinthians 8:11; Hebrews 12:11 RSV.

Encouragement   Psalms 42:11; 1 Thessalonians 5:11.

Faithfulness   Luke 16:10–12.

Get the Facts   Proverbs 14:8, 15; 18:13; 19:2; 23:23; 27:23, 24; Luke 14:31, 32; James 1:5 RSV.

Gospel   Mark 1:15 RSV; John 3:16 RSV; Revelation 3:20 RSV.

Guidance   Psalms 25:4, 5; 32:8 KJV; 143:8; Isaiah 30:21 KJV; Jeremiah 8:4, 5; Mark 1:35.

Investments   Matthew 6:19–21; 24:35 RSV; 25:14–30; Mark 4:19; 2 Timothy 2:4; 2 Peter 3:10.

Partnerships   2 Chronicles 20:35–37; 2 Corinthians 6:14, 15.

Planning   Proverbs 16:1.

Priorities   Joshua 24:15; Proverbs 3:4–6; 11:28; 18:11; 23:4, 5; 24:27; Matthew 6:33 RSV; Romans 1:28, 29; 12:1; 2 Corinthians 8:5; 12:14 PHILLIPS; Philippians 1:21 KJV; 1 Timothy 3:4, 5 RSV; 5:8; 6:10 PHILLIPS; James 1:1 RSV.

Purpose   Romans 8:29; 1 Timothy 6:11.

Saving   Proverbs 21:5, 20; 30:24, 25.

Security   2 Timothy 1:12.

Sharing   Deuteronomy 14:22, 23; Proverbs 3:9, 10; 22:9; 28:27; Malachi 3:8–10; Matthew 6:1–4; 10:42; Mark 9:41; Luke 3:11; 5:3; 6:38 RSV; Romans 12:13; 1 Corinthians 16:2; 2 Corinthians 8:3, 4, 14; 9:6, 7 RSV; 9:11 NEB; Galatians 6:6, 10; James 2:15–17 WUEST.

Source of Wealth   Deuteronomy 8:18 RSV; 2 Chronicles 16:9; Psalms 24:1; 34:9; Proverbs 8:20, 21; Malachi 3:10; Matthew 6:32 COTTON PATCH; 7:7 RSV; 21:22 RSV; John 10:10; 16:24 RSV; Ephesians 3:20 PHILLIPS; Philippians 4:6, 7, 19 RSV.

Speculations   Ecclesiastes 5:15–17; also *see* Investments.

Strength   Psalms 46:10 RSV; Philippians 4:13.

Success   Psalms 1:2, 3.

Unity   Ecclesiastes 4:9; Amos 3:3 KJV; Romans 12:16.

Vision   Proverbs 29:18 KJV; Luke 18:27 RSV; Galatians 6:7, 9 RSV; Revelation 22:11.

Waiting   Psalms 27:14; 40:1–3; Isaiah 40:31 RSV; 52:12, RSV.

Work   Genesis 1:1 RSV; 2:2, 3; Exodus 23:12; 1 Chronicles 28:20; 2 Chronicles 31:21 NAS; Nehemiah 4:6; Proverbs 12:9, 24; 13:11; 13:19 KJV; 14:23; 28:19; Ecclesiastes 5:12; 1 Corinthians 10:31; 14:40; Philippians 2:13 KJV; Colossians 3:23 RSV; 2 Timothy 2:15; 2 Peter 1:10.

Working Wife   Proverbs 31:10, 16.